Vol. 1

1. **WILLIAM HOWARD TAFT**
What Constitutes An Unlawful Trust
Hot Springs, VA (8/5/08)
First issued on Victor 31710
(Courtesy The RCA Records Label, under license from BMG Direct)

2. **WILLIAM HOWARD TAFT**
Democratic Policy Prevents Restoration Of Prosperity
Hot Springs, VA (8/5/08)
First issued on Victor 5555
(Courtesy The RCA Records Label, under license from BMG Direct)

3. **THEODORE ROOSEVELT**
The "Abyssinian Treatment" Of Standard Oil
Emporia, KS (9/22/12)
First issued on Victor 35249
(Courtesy The RCA Records Label, under license from BMG Direct)

4. **THEODORE ROOSEVELT**
Why The Trusts And Bosses Oppose The Progressive Party
Emporia, KS (9/22/12)
First issued on Victor 35250
(Courtesy The RCA Records Label, under license from BMG Direct)

5. **WOODROW WILSON**
The Third Party
New York, NY (9/24/12)
First issued on Victor 35251-A
(Courtesy The RCA Records Label, under license from BMG Direct)

6. **WOODROW WILSON**
To The Farmers
New York, NY (9/24/12)
First issued on Victor 35252-A
(Courtesy The RCA Records Label, under license from BMG Direct)

7. **WARREN G. HARDING**
Americanism
New York, NY (6/29/20)
First issued on Nation's Forum NF 15

8. **WARREN G. HARDING**
Liberty Under The Law
New York, NY (8/6/20)
First issued on Nation's Forum NF 25

9. **WARREN G. HARDING**
Nationalism And Americanism
New York, NY (8/6/20)
Unissued recording made by Nation's Forum [matrix 49878]

10. **CALVIN COOLIDGE**
Inaugural Address (Excerpts)
Washington, DC (3/4/25)
From experimental recordings made by Western Electric [matrices 51775-81]

11. **HERBERT HOOVER**
Radio Address To The Nation On Unemployment Relief
Fort Monroe, VA (10/18/31)
Unissued recording made by Victor [matrix cve 70860-1]
(Courtesy The RCA Records Label, under license from BMG Direct)

All speeches on *Vol. 1* selected by the staff at The Library Of Congress

Vol. 2

1. **FRANKLIN D. ROOSEVELT**
   The First "Fireside Chat" - An Intimate Talk With The People Of The United States On Banking
   Washington, DC (3/12/33)
   (Courtesy Franklin Delano Roosevelt Library)

2. **FRANKLIN D. ROOSEVELT**
   "We Have Only Just Begun To Fight" Campaign Address
   Madison Square Garden, New York, NY (10/31/36)
   (Courtesy Franklin Delano Roosevelt Library)

3. **HARRY S. TRUMAN**
   Address Upon Accepting The Democratic Nomination For President
   Democratic National Convention, Philadelphia, PA (7/15/48)
   (Courtesy Harry S. Truman Library)

   All speeches on *Vol. 2* selected by the staff at The Library Of Congress

Vol. 3

1. **DWIGHT D. EISENHOWER**
   Farewell Radio And Television Address To The American People
   Washington, DC (1/17/61)
   Speech selected by the staff at The Library Of Congress

2. **JOHN F. KENNEDY**
   Commencement Address At American University
   American University, Washington, DC (6/10/63)
   Speech selected by Theodore Sorensen & approved by Jacqueline Bouvier Onassis

3. **LYNDON B. JOHNSON**
   Remarks At The University Of Michigan
   University Of Michigan, Ann Arbor, MI (5/22/64)
   Speech selected by Lady Bird Johnson
   (Courtesy Lyndon Baines Johnson Library)

Vol. 4

1. **RICHARD NIXON**
   Address To The Nation On The War In Vietnam
   Washington, DC (11/3/69)
   Speech selected in accordance with President Nixon's opinion in his book *In The Arena* (Simon & Schuster, 1990)
   (Courtesy Richard Nixon Project)

2. **GERALD R. FORD**
   Remarks On Taking The Oath Of Office
   Washington, DC (8/9/74)
   Speech selected by President Ford
   (Courtesy Gerald R. Ford Library)

3. **JIMMY CARTER**
   "Energy And National Goals" Address To The Nation
   Washington, DC (7/15/79)
   Speech selected by President Carter
   (Courtesy James Earl Carter Center)

Vol. 5

1. RONALD REAGAN
Remarks To The Students And Faculty At Moscow State University
Moscow State University, Moscow, USSR (5/31/88)
Speech selected by President Reagan
(Courtesy National Archives Presidential Library)

2. GEORGE BUSH
Remarks To The Residents Of Leiden
Leiden, The Netherlands (7/17/89)
Speech selected by President Bush
(Courtesy White House & National Archive Presidential Library)

Vol. 6

1. WILLIAM J. CLINTON
Remarks To The Convocation Of The Church Of God In Christ
Memphis, TN (11/13/93)
Speech selected by President Clinton
(Courtesy White House & National Archive Presidential Library)

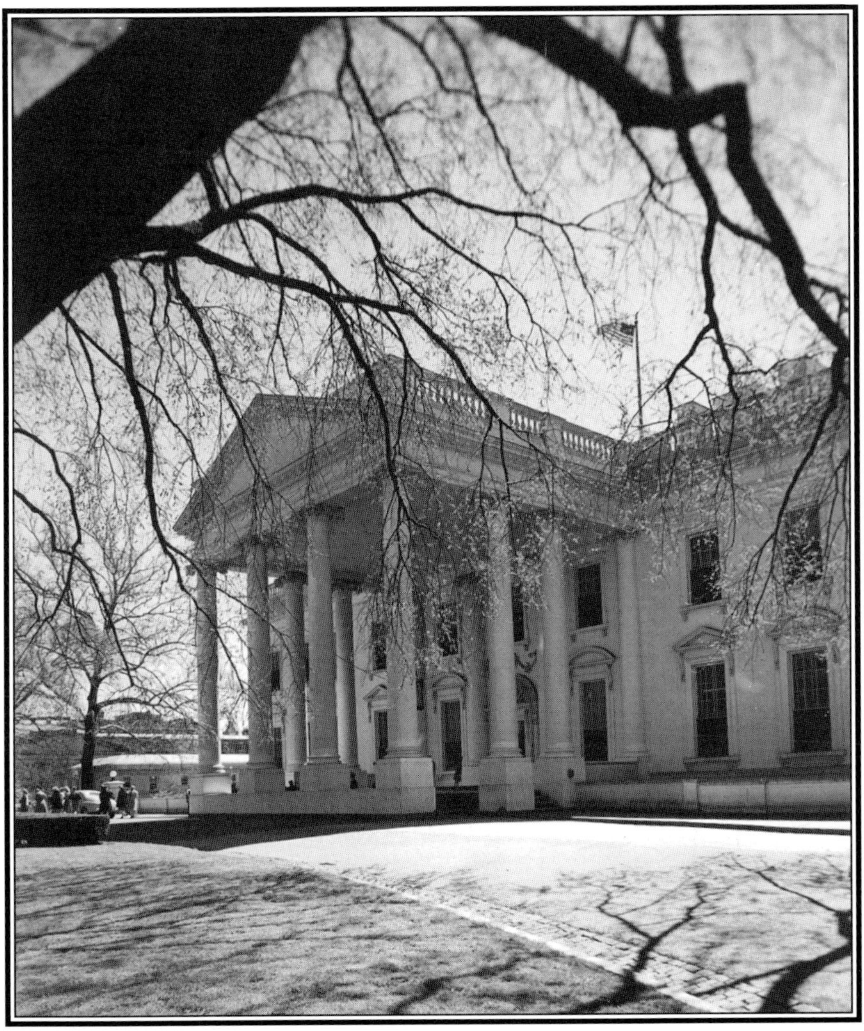

Photo: FPG International

The Library of Congress

is proud to present this aural compilation of 85 years of presidential oratory. To those of us who have never had the opportunity to *hear* the words of 20th century Presidents, particularly those Presidents who served before the era of extended TV coverage, these recordings are a revelation. Here, in their own voices, are 17 of this nation's chief executives — variously sharing their visions, coaxing a nation to support their political programs, and appealing for votes.

We are pleased to have this opportunity to share this small segment of our collections with everyone interested in learning more about our political past and present. In this set, through the Recorded Sound Collections of the Library of Congress Motion Picture, Broadcasting and Recorded Sound Division, you will hear the voices of the recent past as well as of our grandparents' times. You may also gain a sense of the changing role of mass communications in the United States.

Nineteenth century political style was far different from what we see today. One hundred years ago, Presidents did not campaign actively for office; they remained home while surrogates conveyed their views to various political constituencies. Whistle-stop campaigning by rail was thought unseemly, and presidential candidates offered, at most, a few innocuous remarks from their front porches. In the absence of a centralized press, the candidates' inconsistencies in regionally targeted messages were seldom exposed. After election, the President occasionally sent messages to Congress, as in the case of the annual state of the union address, but these compositions were read to the Congress by clerks, not by the incumbent himself.

The 20th century changed all this. It became acceptable for presidential candidates to travel widely and engage a diverse electorate directly. The relationship between the President and Congress also shifted. Woodrow Wilson broke a century of precedent when he became the first President since John Adams to address joint sessions of Congress in person with messages of national import. Oratory for the first time became an important weapon in a President's political armory. The discs in this set, therefore, offer a unique opportunity not only to hear voices from the past, but to consider changes in oratorical styles.

"The Missing Link Supplied"

The novelty of presidential candidates recording their stump speeches in 1908 led cartoonist J. S. Pughe to draw this cartoon for Puck *magazine. The dummy hand for shaking attached to the phonograph supplies the missing link that would make personal appearances by politicians obsolete — an ironic foreshadowing of the importance of mass media in election campaigns.*

The first recordings were acoustical; that is, they were produced by a speaker talking into a studio-recording device that mechanically transmitted sound to a stylus, which then grooved a wax disc. The early recordings in this anthology were made that way. The first presidential voice heard is that of William Howard Taft, recorded during the campaign of 1908. Both Taft and his opponent, William Jennings Bryan, recorded messages on wax discs that were reproduced and shipped around the country and played at church meetings, campaign rallies, and public forums. For the first time a widely dispersed electorate was able to hear the voices (or at least the acoustical impress) of national political candidates.

Acoustical pressings were the norm until the birth of electrical recording in 1925. This technology enabled a recording engineer to capture inflection and nuance and, occasionally, the background noise of the crowds to provide a more visceral sense of a President's impact. The power of the "bully pulpit," as the presidency was described by Theodore Roosevelt, was enhanced by the advent of radio. The popular Andrew Jackson reached no more than the 10,000 persons gathered for his inauguration in 1829. One hundred years later, Warren Harding was heard by 125,000 people. But in 1925, Calvin Coolidge broadcast a speech to 23 million listeners.

Television followed in the 1940s and 1950s. Today mass communications allow us to witness legislative debates as they occur and to see and hear Presidents as they speak. This collection will enable listeners to turn to the speeches of the past and to recapture the immediacy of special moments in our nation's history.

—*James H. Billington*
The Librarian of Congress

How the Speeches Were Selected

The editors of this set of speeches have attempted to present a complete speech from every U.S. President whose voice has been recorded. This has not been entirely possible. In 1878 Thomas Edison demonstrated his new invention, the "speaking phonograph," at the White House and recorded President Rutherford B. Hayes. That recording, on tinfoil — the fragile medium of the embryonic Edison recording machine — is lost. William Howard Taft's 1908 campaign addresses, which open this set, were thought to be the oldest presidential recordings in existence, but even they may not be the first. Benjamin Harrison is believed to have recorded for the Bettini cylinder company, but no verified copy of his recording is extant. We do know that the many existing turn-of-the-century recordings labeled "President McKinley's Last Speech" are not of William McKinley. The three major record companies of the day — Columbia, Edison, and Victor — all issued recordings of the address President McKinley gave at the Pan-American Exposition in Buffalo, New York, the day before he was assassinated. None of these records were actually made by President McKinley; most, if not all, were recorded by the prolific early recording star Len Spencer. Often, however, the labels of those McKinley recordings did not identify who was speaking. They did not falsely state that it was McKinley, but they did not say it was Spencer either.

The opening recordings of William Howard Taft were selected from the series of 13 sides he recorded for the Victor Talking Machine Company in the summer of 1908. He also recorded speeches for Columbia and Edison, as did his opponent, William Jennings Bryan. It is unlikely that any of these sides, all individually titled, were originally self-contained speeches. The 78-rpm discs of that day could include, at most, only five minutes of sound per side. These recordings are thematically self-

Louder Bill!
Theodore Roosevelt chose not to run for reelection in 1908. Yet, according to this August 1908 New York Herald cartoon by W. A. Rogers, the President didn't refrain from offering Republican candidate William Howard Taft advice. In this case, the advice contradicts the President's adage "Speak softly and carry a big stick."

contained excerpts from Taft's standard stump speeches. This is the case, too, with the speeches included here of Theodore Roosevelt, Woodrow Wilson, and Warren Harding. The only recordings in existence of these three Presidents are from series made for commercial companies as part of their election efforts. Either because it was too awkward and inconvenient to make these mechanical recordings (recorded before the development of microphones and amplifiers), or because neither the politicians nor the record companies saw a market for Presidents' voices, we know of no other commercial sound recordings made by these men.

Radio — its new audiences and its associated technologies — changed that. The Calvin Coolidge inaugural address included here was recorded from radio lines — albeit only partially. Coolidge's successor, Herbert Hoover, understood the potential reach of radio and used it; Franklin Roosevelt mastered the medium. Their broadcasts and those of their successors were recorded and preserved by radio and television audiences, stations, and networks. From the thousands of existing recordings of these broadcasts, the editors of this set made selections guided by the goal of best conveying each President's style, programs, and philosophies. Franklin Roosevelt, who was elected to office four times and served more than 12 years, is represented by two complete speeches on this set: a fireside chat done in an "intimate" radio style; and a speech delivered to a political convention of thousands.

All of the earlier speeches on this disc — from William Howard Taft to Dwight D. Eisenhower — were chosen by staff at the Library of Congress. The choice of speeches to be included for John F. Kennedy and his successors was made by the Presidents themselves, their widows, or their associates. The Librarian of Congress asked each what single speech or speeches they wanted to assure would be preserved and made available to students of history and government. A response was received from every President's office, with the exception of Richard Nixon's. The selection of his "Silent Majority" speech for inclusion in this set was made on the basis of his own writing about the speech. The support for this project of the Presidents, the presidential libraries, and their associates is greatly appreciated.

—*Samuel Brylawski*

Samuel Brylawski is the recorded sound specialist at the Library of Congress Motion Picture, Broadcasting and Recorded Sound Division. He also writes and lectures frequently on radio and American popular music. He first conceived of publishing this set of speeches when, as a reference librarian at the Library of Congress, he noted that the in-print availability of Presidents' speeches on record was nearly entirely limited to inaugural addresses.

This set of speeches is a study in the exercise of power through language — a microcosm of moments in which, in the words of Franklin D. Roosevelt, Presidents and presidential aspirants acted as "leaders of thought at times when certain historic ideas in the life of the nation had to be clarified."[1]

The selections in this set feature Presidents and presidential candidates in multiple settings with various demands. The genres represented here include both the rhetoric of the campaign and that of governance. Included among the stump speeches delivered in the heat of campaigns are those by William Howard Taft, Theodore Roosevelt, Woodrow Wilson, Herbert Hoover, and FDR. Truman's speech accepting his party's nomination in 1948 represents this form.

The genres of governance are represented as well. The inaugural, the speech forecasting a presidency, is given by Coolidge. From Gerald Ford we hear its unique equivalent, an address made after he was sworn in to replace the only President in the nation's history to resign, Richard Nixon. The farewell, the other speech that brackets many presidencies, is here delivered by Eisenhower.

Where the inaugural forecasts principles and the farewell recaps accomplishments, the policy speech articulates a plan of action. The ceremonial occasion of the commencement address created the occasion for two important policy speeches included in the set: John Kennedy's speech on disarmament at American University in 1963 and Lyndon Johnson's preview of the Great Society at the University of Michigan in 1964.

The speech to the nation, a genre made possible by the advent of the broadcast media, also provided important occasions for presidential statement. Included here are FDR's calming fireside chat explaining his actions to stabilize the banks, and Nixon's televised address reiterating the "Nixon Doctrine."

The collection features another significant address to the American people, Carter's "Crisis Of Energy" speech of 1979. Where Nixon's televised address on "The Silent Majority" focused on international affairs, Carter's addressed domestic concerns.

Speeches delivered to audiences outside the United States suggest the importance of the President's role as a world leader. Both Reagan's speech at Moscow State University in 1988 and Bush's in Leiden, the Netherlands, in 1989 speak *of* and *to* a world in transition.

We listen to the speeches of the past through the filter of time not foreseen when the discourse was crafted or spoken. We know that Hoover's optimism that the nation will soon pass through its Valley Forge to its Yorktown proved unjustified. As we hear Johnson's call in May 1964 to "join in the battle to build the Great Society" and his castigation of those "timid souls who say this battle cannot be won," we remember that the battle that would preoccupy the country during his tenure would instead be one against North Vietnam. We hear FDR's claims about peace in 1936 and know that the country would soon be engulfed in a war not envisioned in the pledge "I submit to you a record of peace; and on that record a well-founded expectation for future peace . . . ."

Throughout this collection we also hear the phrases that define our remembrance of our country's past:

From Coolidge, "America seeks no earthly empire built on blood and force. No ambition, no temptation, lures her to thought of foreign domination."

From FDR, "The nation knows that I hate war, and I know that the nation hates war."

From Truman, "By indirection, the 80th Congress has tried to sabotage the power policies the United States has pursued for 14 years."

From Eisenhower, "In the councils of government, we must guard against the acquisition of unwarranted influence, whether sought or unsought, by the military-industrial complex."

From Kennedy, "I speak of peace, therefore, as the necessary rational end of rational men."

From LBJ, "For in your time we have the opportunity to move not only toward the rich society and the powerful society, but upward to the Great Society."

From Nixon, "The defense of freedom is everybody's business, not just America's business. And it is particularly the responsibility of the people whose freedom is threatened." And from the same speech, "And so tonight — to you, the great silent majority of my fellow Americans — I ask for your support."

From Ford, "My fellow Americans, our long national nightmare is over. Our Constitution works; our great republic is a government of laws and not of men."

From Carter, "The threat is nearly invisible in ordinary ways. It is a crisis of confidence. It is a crisis that strikes at the very heart and soul and spirit of our national will."

From Clinton: "I have worked hard to keep faith with our common efforts: to restore the economy; to reserve the politics of helping only those at the top of our totem pole and not the hard-working middle class or the poor; to bring our people together across racial and regional and political lines; to make a strength out of our diversity instead of letting it tear us apart; to reward work and family and community and try to move us forward into the 21st century. I have tried to keep faith."

The stylistic imprint of each President is evident in the selected speeches. Hoover's language was awkward, even as he addressed the failure of words. "I would that I possessed the art of words to fix the real issue with which the troubled world is faced in the mind and heart of every American man and woman."

Truman used plain, even blunt speech at the nominating convention. ". . . it was such a rotten bill," he says of the price control legislation sent to his desk, "that I couldn't sign it. And 30 days after that, they sent me one just as bad." From Nixon, precise forecasts of key ideas.

Kennedy carefully balanced phrases, as in, "Peace need not be impracticable, and war need not be inevitable." Reagan was comfortable with anecdote and humor — a tendency evident when he recounted a folk tale about the angel who invests each baby with special attributes by kissing a portion of the child's body. Considering a bureaucrat, the woman in the tale says, "I've been trying to figure out where the angel kissed you so that you should sit there for so long and do nothing."

The addresses reflect not only differences among the individuals delivering them, but changes in the culture as well. In early addresses, Presidents assume a comfortable familiarity with the Old and New Testaments; Hoover says in an October 1931 campaign address, "Modern society cannot survive with the defense of Cain, 'Am I my brother's keeper?'" Two generations later, Reagan can assume that even in Moscow students will understand the meanings to be drawn from his reference to *Butch Cassidy And The Sundance Kid*."

With the presidency of Woodrow Wilson came a changed conception of the role of presidential rhetoric, as well. Some previous Presidents, he opined, had functioned as if "there should be no intimate communication of any kind between the Capitol and the White House; that the President as a man was no more at liberty to lead the Congress by persuasion than he was at liberty as President to dominate them by authority."[2] As President, Wilson would resume personal, oral delivery of the State of the Union Address to Congress, a practice the weak-voiced Thomas Jefferson had discontinued.

In more recent times, speechmaking became a staple activity of Presidents. From Truman through Reagan, the number of speeches delivered by a president rose[3], although the number of major speeches delivered by a President in a given year has remained steady at four or five.[4] Modern Presidents have recognized the power of such addresses to blunt a slide in the polls or boost popular support. By comparing months in which a major speech is given with those in which one is not, scholars have concluded that a speech can account for a three-percent difference in the polls.[5]

An important speech affects the President as well as the public. "When I was President," recalled Richard Nixon, "I found that preparing a major speech was a very effective discipline, not only for bringing policy decisions to a head, but also for refining my own thinking."[6] "It is much easier," noted JFK, "to make speeches than it is to finally make the judgments, because unfortunately your advisers are frequently divided."[7]

Despite the differences in topic, genre, and audience, there are fundamental continuities among the speeches. By recalling the words of their predecessors, Presidents remind us of the underlying stability of American institutions, and suggest as well that Presidents draw lessons from history. Some recall durable principles. Reagan, for example, reminds the students in Moscow of Washington's farewell words: "Reason and experience both forbid us to expect that national morality can prevail in exclusion of religious principle. And it is absolutely true that virtue of morality is a necessary spring of popular government."

Others, including John Kennedy and Richard Nixon, amend memorable phrases to reflect changing times. Where Wilson sought to make the world safe for democracy, Kennedy asks at American University that we "help make the world safe for diversity." In the "Silent Majority" speech, Nixon suggests that Wilson's dream of a war to end war "was shattered on the hard realities of great power politics, and Woodrow Wilson died a broken man." "Tonight," Nixon adds, "I do not tell you that the war in Vietnam is the war to end wars. But I do say this: I have initiated a plan which will end this war in a way that will bring us closer to that great goal to which Woodrow Wilson and every American President in our history has been dedicated — the goal of a just and lasting peace."

There is substantive continuity as well. In Eisenhower's farewell we hear that "Disarmament, with mutual honor and confidence, is a continuing imperative. Together we must learn how to compose differences, not with arms, but with intellect and decent purpose." And in one of the most moving passages in the speech, the former general adds, "As one who has

President Woodrow Wilson speaking in Long Beach, New Jersey, 1916.

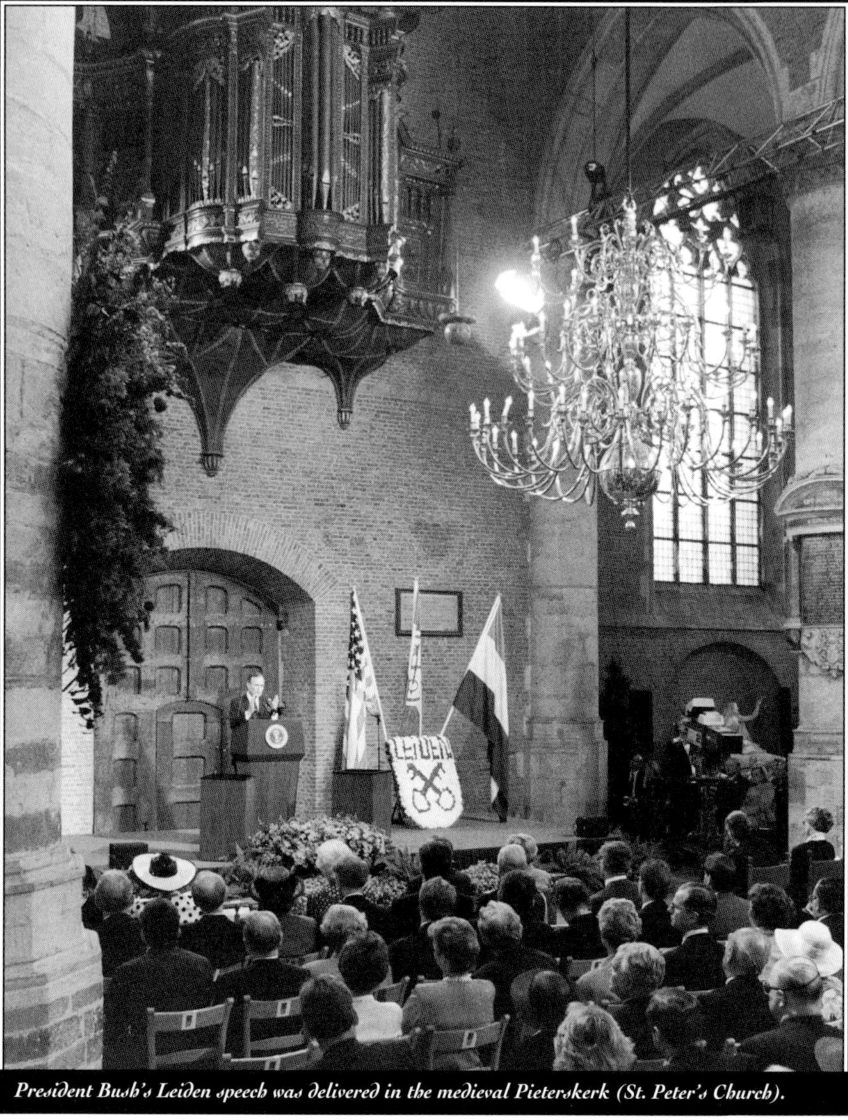

Photo: Bush Presidential Materials Project

President Bush's Leiden speech was delivered in the medieval Pieterskerk (St. Peter's Church).

witnessed the horror and the lingering sadness of war — as one who knows that another war could utterly destroy this civilization which has so slowly and painfully built over thousands of years — I wish I could say tonight that a lasting peace is in sight."

Three years later, in what many regard as the finest speech of his presidency — the commencement address at American University — John Kennedy declares that the U.S. would suspend nuclear tests in the atmosphere "as long as other states do not do so. We will not be the first to resume." The speech also announces the beginning of discussions in Moscow on a comprehensive test-ban treaty. "We are both devoting massive sums of money to weapons that could be better devoted to combating ignorance, poverty, and disease," Kennedy says. "We are both caught up in a vicious and dangerous cycle in which suspicion on one side breeds suspicion on the other, and new weapons beget counterweapons. In short, the United States and its allies, and the Soviet Union and its allies, have a mutually deep interest in a just and genuine agreement."

The work of Presidents of both parties made it possible in 1988 for Ronald Reagan to tell the students at Moscow State University, "Just a few years ago, few would have imagined the progress our two nations have made together. The INF treaty, which General Secretary Gorbachev and I signed last December in Washington and whose instruments of ratification we will exchange tomorrow — the first true nuclear arms reduction treaty in history, calling for the elimination of an entire class of U.S. and Soviet nuclear missiles."

The battle over taxation is as perennial a theme as the search for peace. To those following the debates in the current Congress, the following passages, the first from Coolidge in 1925, the second from Truman in 1948, have a contemporary ring.

"The time is arriving when we can have further tax reduction, when, unless we wish to hamper the people in their right to earn a living, we must have tax reform. The method of raising revenue ought not to impede the transaction of business; it ought to encourage it."

"Now everybody likes to have low taxes, but we must reduce the national debt in times of prosperity. And when tax relief can be given, it ought to go to those who need it most, and not those who need it least, as this Republican rich man's tax bill did when they passed it over my veto on the third try."

Powerful rhetoric often draws impact from its setting. Johnson defines the Great Society in the place where the peace corps was started, and Clinton's 1993 speech in Memphis draws much of its power from the fact that it occurred at the Memphis Mason Temple, where Martin Luther King Jr. delivered the last sermon before his death. That place invests with special meaning Clinton's claim that "The freedom to die before you are a teenager is not what Martin Luther King lived and died for." In a house of worship calls to moral action have added resonance. "It is our moral duty," says Clinton, "to turn it around."

In another fusion of words and place, Bush chose Leiden, The Netherlands, as the site from which to define the lessons of the post-Cold War era. The reason? Leiden is "a city whose very name has symbolized for centuries Dutch determination and the struggle for freedom against the forces of occupation. And for Americans, too, Leiden is a special city, a place where we trace our origins. So many of the individuals who shaped the modern world walked the cobbled streets of Leiden. And it was here that Hugo de Groot, known to the world as Grotius, the father of modern international law, studied in the nation that is today the home of the International Court of Justice. And it was here that Rembrandt lived and worked and created a world of beauty that moves us still today. And it was here to Leiden that the Pilgrims came to escape persecution — to live, work, and worship in peace . . ." They left Leiden for America on the same mission.

As American political discourse moved from the stump to the living room, it became increasingly personal and conversational. Fiery oratory gave way to the fireside chat. Where the stump invited exhortation, explanation was a more natural mode in the intimacy of a living room. "I want to talk for a few minutes with the people of the United States about banking . . ." FDR says in his March 12, 1933, fireside chat. "I want to tell you what has been done in the last few days, why it was done, and what the next steps are going to be." His reason? "It was my endeavor to explain these things in non-technical language," FDR wrote later, "so that the great mass of our citizens who had little or no experience with the technicalities of banking would be relieved of their anxiety as to whether they would ever see their money again."[8] The public responded. Where more than seven and a half billion dollars were in circulation in March, 1933, one and a quarter billion of it had moved back into the banks by the end of that month.[9]

FDR's successor was less adept in handling the new technology. "I am sorry that the microphones are in the way," notes Truman in opening his 1948 acceptance address, "but I must leave them the way they are . . ." His awareness of the microphones — which called for a softer, more conversational delivery to the radio listeners at home — is short-lived. Within minutes Truman is back in stump style shouting into the nation's living rooms — a prospect made even less palatable by the fact that the speech was being delivered at 2 a.m. Eastern standard time.

FDR perfected the conversational style on radio in his fireside chats as Reagan did in the age of television. Only when he repronounces a word or falters on a line are we aware that Reagan is delivering from text. It is that talent that invests the words of the Moscow speech with power when he says, "I've been told that there's a popular song in your country — perhaps you know it — whose evocative refrain asks the question, 'Do the Russians want a war?' In answer it says, 'Go ask that silence lingering in the air, above the birch and poplar there; beneath those trees the soldiers lie. Go ask my mother, ask my wife; then you will have to ask no more, 'Do the Russians want a war?'"

By contrast, Herbert Hoover's delivery of what could have been a memorable peroration is flat, uninspired, and as a result, inconclusive. "I am on my way to participate in the commemoration of the victory of Yorktown," he says. "It is a name which brings a glow of pride to every American. It recalls the final victory of our people after years of sacrifice and privation. This nation passed through Valley Forge and came to Yorktown."

The broadcast media affected both the prose of Presidents and the personalization of their public discourse. Where the earlier speeches in this set speak impersonally, the later ones, particularly those by Ford, Carter, and Clinton, are highly personal. The number of times a president says "I" increases in the later speeches.

The transformations heard in the style and tone of the speeches are in part a function of evolving technology. Early presidential discourse sounds distant and flat because it was being broadcast by shortwave or recorded on wax disc. As technology evolved, the fidelity of the sound improved. Contemporary speeches, broadcast to America's television sets, sound as if they are being delivered a few feet away.

Yet even the crudest technology represented here has transported our President's thoughts through time to us. Through another recording format, the CD, this collection of speeches invites us to re-experience some of the major moments of the 20th century, captured in sound.

—*Kathleen Hall Jamieson*

Kathleen Hall Jamieson is a professor and dean of the Annenberg School for Communication of the University of Pennsylvania and author of Eloquence In An Electronic Age *(Oxford: 1988);* Packaging The Presidency *(Oxford: 1984, 1992, 1996);* Dirty Politics *(Oxford: 1992); and* Beyond The Double Bind: Women And Leadership *(Oxford: 1995).*

1. Quoted by George C. Edwards III, *The Public Presidency* (New York: St. Martin's Press, 1983), p. 38.
2. Wilson, *Constitutional Government* (New York: Columbia University Press, 1908), p. 70.
3. Roderick Hart, *The Sound Of Leadership* (Chicago: University of Chicago Press, 1987), p. 11.
4. Barbara Hinckley, *The Symbolic Presidency* (New York and London: Routledge, 1990), p. 19.
5. Hinckley, p. 25. See also: Lyn Ragsdale, "The Politics Of Presidential Speechmaking, 1949-1980" *American Political Science Review* (December 1984), pp. 971-84.
6. Richard Nixon, *Leaders* (New York: Simon and Schuster, 1982), p. 346.
7. Year-End Conversation With The President, Washington D.C., December 17, 1962, in *Let The Word Go Forth: The Speeches, Statements, And Writings Of John F. Kennedy, 1947 To 1963*, Selected by Theodore C. Sorensen (New York: Delacorte Press, 1988), p. 31.
8. Franklin D. Roosevelt, *The Public Papers And Addresses Of Franklin D. Roosevelt*, Vol. 2 (New York: Random House, 1938), p. 60.
9. *Ibid.*, p. 65.

This series of recordings

presents the voices of our national leaders from Theodore Roosevelt to Bill Clinton — monuments in sound. It is no small feat to have preserved their actual voices. From these voices we gain some measure of the men themselves. However, the recordings can be used in many interesting ways. We present this aural swath of 20th-century American history to give listeners first-hand evidence of the power, presentation, and purpose of the men in whom Americans have vested the highest position available in our country. Here, across time, they speak to us about their dreams for our future — and, at times, their own personal futures as well.

A recording of a political speech is a fixed moment in time. As a politician makes a speech, he or she not only voices a personal ideology, but also responds to whatever was important at that particular moment; for example, a recent attack by the opposition, news that he was leading (or behind) in the polls, or the need to raise campaign funds without offending a significant constituency. Each speech conjures up a specific time and place. Listening to these speeches, we can reconstruct not only what was going on during the election, but what interested the candidates and Presidents at that moment.

It is striking how similar the speeches are. Throughout this century, they raise two broad issues: First, how deeply will the federal government become involved in domestic affairs? Second, as America grows in power and stature, how will it fulfill its role abroad?

These issues are paramount in the first recordings in this set, made in August of 1908, as William Howard Taft, then a candidate against William Jennings Bryan, discusses tariffs on trade, labor disputes, and — ten years after the Spanish-American War — America's treatment of Cuba and the Philippines. The same issues are also paramount in the recordings by both Ronald Reagan and George Bush, discussing the benefits of a *laissez-faire* system and America's role abroad. Both issues involve how the U.S. federal government uses its power, and when the exercise of this power ceases to be benevolent and becomes overly intrusive.

Presidential responses to these issues have, of course, varied throughout this century. One of the most remarkable things that these speeches show is how fast the country can swing from a progressive mood to a conservative one, how in eight years the country can go from Wilson to Harding, from Roosevelt to Eisenhower, from progressivism to a complete distrust of experimentation.

The Influence of the Media

On another level, these recordings can be studied to understand how the media have influenced presidential speeches, the relationship between the government and its citizens, and the nature of the presidency itself.

Democracy itself owes a large debt to the development of the printing press and the resulting easy dissemination of ideas (try to imagine American politics without a newspaper, especially before radio or television). One reason the Framers chose an indirect system of election (the Electoral College) for the presidency was the absence of a national community of debate and discourse. There were no newspapers of national circulation in 1787 and, hence, no informed basis for a single national decision on who would be the best President. The development of a fast, efficient railroad system also had a powerful effect on the American political system in the 19th century, making possible the barnstorming presidential campaign. Traveling by train, a candidate could make a speech one night in Chicago, the next in Des Moines, the next in Kansas City. William Jennings Bryan was the first campaigner to rely heavily on the whistle-stop; in 1900, he made more than 600 speeches in 24 states in less than three months.[1] This kind of campaign made charisma — the personal magnetism that could create a new sort of political devotion to a candidate — increasingly important.

For the first time, a large number of voters could actually see, hear, and compare the candidates.

And waiting in the wings at the beginning of the 20th century were the new inventions, the moving picture and the phonograph. Political candidates quickly saw their advantages.

The first part of this collection contains speeches not by Presidents, but by presidential candidates. Although Theodore Roosevelt was President from 1901-1908, before William Howard Taft (1909-1913), Taft precedes Roosevelt on the set because the phonograph records were made by the candidates *when they were campaigning*. Once in office, they rarely made recordings. It is likely that only the heat of a presidential election provided enough of a potential market to induce a company to record and issue a presidential speech. Thus this set contains no speeches by Presidents in office before 1925 and the advent of radio. The collection begins with Taft, the 27th President, because while Roosevelt preceded Taft as President, he did not make recordings until 1912, when he was campaigning on the Progressive or "Bull Moose" ticket.

William Howard Taft and the Campaign of 1908

The shadow of the 1904 campaign hung heavily over 1908. William Howard Taft was the handpicked successor of Theodore Roosevelt, whom Roosevelt expected to carry on his policies intact. The Democrats, remembering the poor showing of Judge Alton Parker, their drab 1904 candidate, decided to once again nominate the flamboyant William Jennings Bryan, now running for the third time. Bryan campaigned against the monopolistic trusts and banks and called for a downward revision of the high protective tariff. Like Bryan, Taft, too, pledged moderate reform, in accordance with the previous Roosevelt administration — but not too much reform. Taft, too, attacked the trusts and asserted that labor had the right to organize, to strike, and to use peaceful means to attain its ends. However, he believed that boycotts against businesses that bought nonunion goods and against "closed shops" were illegal. Taft originally campaigned against ex parte injunctions, used legally to enjoin strikes, but then wavered on the issue after strong pressure from industrialists. This provoked organized labor's move away from the Republican Party. On the other hand, Taft annoyed big business but pleased small-business interests when, in response to pressure from Bryan, he supported a downward revision of the tariff.

The election year 1908 was also the first in which sound recordings were prominent. The first presidential candidate to record campaign speeches himself to make them available commercially was the great speaker William Jennings Bryan, in May of 1908. Although Bryan ran for President three times, he was never elected; and for that reason, his recordings are not included here. Just as Bryan's political ideas were appropriated by political opponents, his pioneering use of the phonograph record influenced presidential candidates and Presidents for years to come. On August 3, 1908, William Howard Taft — attending the Virginia Bar Association meeting in Hot Springs, Virginia — made a series of recordings incorporating parts of his acceptance speech given in Cincinnati, Ohio, on July 28, 1908.[2] Selections from these records are heard on this set. When he heard that Taft had made recordings, Bryan commented:

> The Republican papers have been making fun of me for using the phonograph as a means of reaching the public, but since the Republican candidate has followed the example, I presume that the criticism will cease, and that this will now be regarded as a dignified method of discussing public questions. It looks as if the Democrats were going to have a hard

time this year protecting their patents from infringement.³

While the records of Bryan and Taft were sold to the public, they were also used another way: Supporters would schedule a meeting in a church hall or town meeting place and invite the public to hear the voice of the candidate from the morning-glory horn of a record player. Many Americans still did not own record players, and the sound of the actual candidate's voice coming to them must have been an unbelievable thrill.

However, the phonograph may have helped Taft more than Bryan in 1908. Although Bryan's 1896 "Cross Of Gold" speech may be the single most famous American political address, his recordings are not really more effective than those of Taft. Part of Bryan's problem was the acoustical recording process of the time.

In the acoustical method, speakers such as Bryan, Theodore Roosevelt, or Warren G. Harding spoke into a large horn, and the resulting sound waves moved a diaphragm, driving a stylus which made grooves in a wax master disc. No electricity was used. In the acoustical method, many of the harmonics and overtones were completely lost, and some of the other sound waves, especially extreme high and low frequencies, could not be heard. Acoustical recording meant, in addition, that these speeches were not "actualities," documentary recordings made on the scene. The records usually had to be made in a studio, under hothouse conditions, away from the cheering crowds that do so much to excite a passionate speaker. The acoustical method meant that a florid, expressive speaker like Bryan, who could raise crowds to a fever pitch of excitement, lost much of his power in the recording process. On the other hand, a crisp, matter-of-fact, legally trained speaker like Taft may have benefitted by comparison. The limitations of the media would make a difference in politics. One might wonder what would have happened in the 1908 campaign if Bryan had made electrical recordings, or, for that matter, if the 350-pound Taft had appeared on television.

The use of the phonograph in the presidential campaign of 1908 struck the public imagination. There were many jokes and political cartoons about the record campaign. Several cities, such as Spokane and Des Moines, had record duels. At a duel in Spokane on September 30, 1908,

William Howard Taft speaking at the Louisiana Purchase Exposition, St. Louis, 1904.

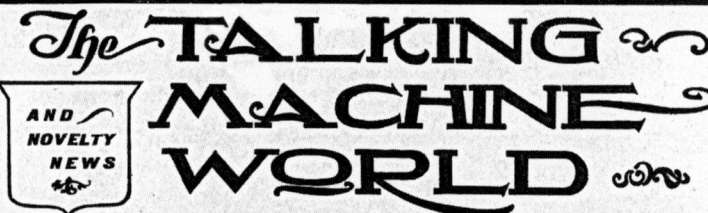

Presidential candidates William Howard Taft and William Jennings Bryan recorded campaign speeches for the 1908 election for all three of the major record companies of the day: Victor, Columbia, and Edison. Columbia advertised its new Taft records (on cylinder as well as disc) on the cover of the September 15, 1908, Talking Machine World.

Frank L. Graham, a spokesman for Bryan, and George W. Leonard, a supporter of Taft, engaged in a battle of recordings for hours. The Spokane paper describes part of the duel as Graham was playing part of a Bryan record:

"*This tariff plank of the Denver convention not only demands —*" [from the recording].

But the voice never finished the sentence, as Leonard started full blast with the "Merry Ha Ha" song, which scored, and he followed this with Taft's declaration that the

Democratic Party represents the restoration of prosperity, adding: "*Such a course as taking the tariff off on all articles coming into competition with the so-called trusts would not only destroy the trusts, but all of their smaller competitors.*"

Graham responded with the chorus of Murray K. Hill's droll song, "Oh, glory!" in which the Bryanites joined with vigor.

The Leonard [Taft] cylinder was well into the judge's review of the progress of the peoples of our foreign dependencies when the din ceased, and before another interruption came, the phonograph had spouted these words:

"*It would be cowardly to lay down the burden of bringing education and happiness to the millions of people until our purpose is achieved.*"

"Imperialism!" cried an excited man, as Graham reached for a fresh record, adding, "Let's hear what Bill Bryan says about that . . ."[4]

With or without the ballyhoo, these duels were effective because of popular interest in the recordings of presidential campaign speeches. The candidates quickly recognized the value of this new tool.

President Theodore Roosevelt speaking in Evanston, Illinois, 1903.

Theodore Roosevelt, Woodrow Wilson, and the Campaign of 1912

In 1912 all three major presidential contestants used recordings. Taft, once again the Republican candidate, made another series of discs for the Victor Talking Machine Company at Beverly, Massachusetts, on October 1, 1912. Theodore Roosevelt, the third-party Progressive candidate, took a day off from his western whistle-stop campaign, and on September 22, 1912, at the Whitley Hotel in Emporia, Kansas, recorded the series of speeches that are heard here. In Kansas, Roosevelt was staying with William Allen White, the celebrated journalist, who explained to a reporter:

"[The recordings] will be sent into the country districts, and when the sheriff and register of deeds go out to the schoolhouse at 9-Mile Corners to hold a political meeting, they will take a talking machine along, and Roosevelt will give them a speech."[5]

Woodrow Wilson also used the new medium and recorded a series of records in New York. It should be noted that Wilson also commissioned a film about himself for his campaign.

The Trust Buster

Taft, Roosevelt, and Wilson all opposed the trusts — for different reasons, and to different degrees. In fact, more anti-trust cases had been instituted under Taft's administration than that of Theodore Roosevelt. However, Taft, the conservative Republican candidate, was not anxious to offend his supporters; hence, in the campaign his voice was muted. Roosevelt had been coaxed back into politics by

President Woodrow Wilson, April 1916.

progressives disappointed with Taft, and he advocated ever more radical policies as the candidate of his new Progressive or Bull Moose party. The "trust buster" not only continued to oppose the evils of big business, he advocated the strengthening of the federal government to closely regulate business and the economy and initiate more social reforms. His government would become far larger, stronger, and — in the eyes of his Republican ex-supporters — more intrusive.

Roosevelt on these discs makes the most of his popular trust-busting reputation with the voters, especially with his baiting of "Archbold and Penrose." John Dustin Archbold had become the head of Standard Oil, the trust which was the epitome of everything that was wrong with trusts in the eyes of many Americans. Boies Penrose was the chairman of the Republican State Committee of Pennsylvania and one of the most powerful figures in the party. At the convention of 1912, Penrose supported Taft. In 1904 Penrose had asked Archbold and Standard Oil for a campaign contribution of $25,000. Standard Oil gave him the money and also gave the Republican National Committee $100,000. A scandal resulted, and a Senate subcommittee convened to investigate irregularities in campaign contributions. Testifying before it on August 23, 1912, Archbold complained bitterly, "Darkest Abyssinia never saw anything like the course of treatment which we [Standard Oil] experienced at the hands of the administration following Mr. Roosevelt's election in 1904."[6] Roosevelt, with great relish, takes Archbold's statement and promises to apply the "Abyssinian treatment" to other wrongdoers. His promise is heard on this set.

In 1912 Woodrow Wilson took a more Jeffersonian position, in opposition to Roosevelt's interventionist policies. Wilson opposed the strengthening of the federal government, and rather took the position that the trusts should be broken up into smaller, more competitive units to restore what he felt was the classic American system. This is the central debate between Wilson and Roosevelt in Roosevelt's speech "The Power Of The People" and Wilson's speech "The Third Party." Wilson won the election, but today, more than 80 years later, the debate is far from over.

Warren Harding and the Campaign of 1920

In 1920, after World War I, the mood of the country was conservative, and few could have addressed this mood better than the Republican Warren G. Harding. Harding, with his running mate Calvin Coolidge, ran against James M. Cox and vice-presidential candidate Franklin D. Roosevelt. Among the issues were prohibition, the tariff, and American membership in the League of Nations. After being nominated, Harding retreated to his home in Marion, Ohio, from which he conducted the "Front Porch Campaign." However, on June 29, 1920, only a few days after being nominated, he made a recording entitled "Americanism," attacking America's proposed entry into the League of Nations. The speech, included here, was designed to be circulated on July 4, but was criticized by the *New York Times* two days after it was recorded:

In a Horn
Mr. Harding's first campaign speech was declaimed into the horn of a recording phonograph. The faithful instrument will proclaim it through the land on Independence Day. We cannot undertake to predict what the Republican candidate's countrymen will make of it. We are more concerned with its effect on William Howard Taft, who has gallantly assumed the task of proving that under the coming Republican Administration the Treaty will be ratified and the

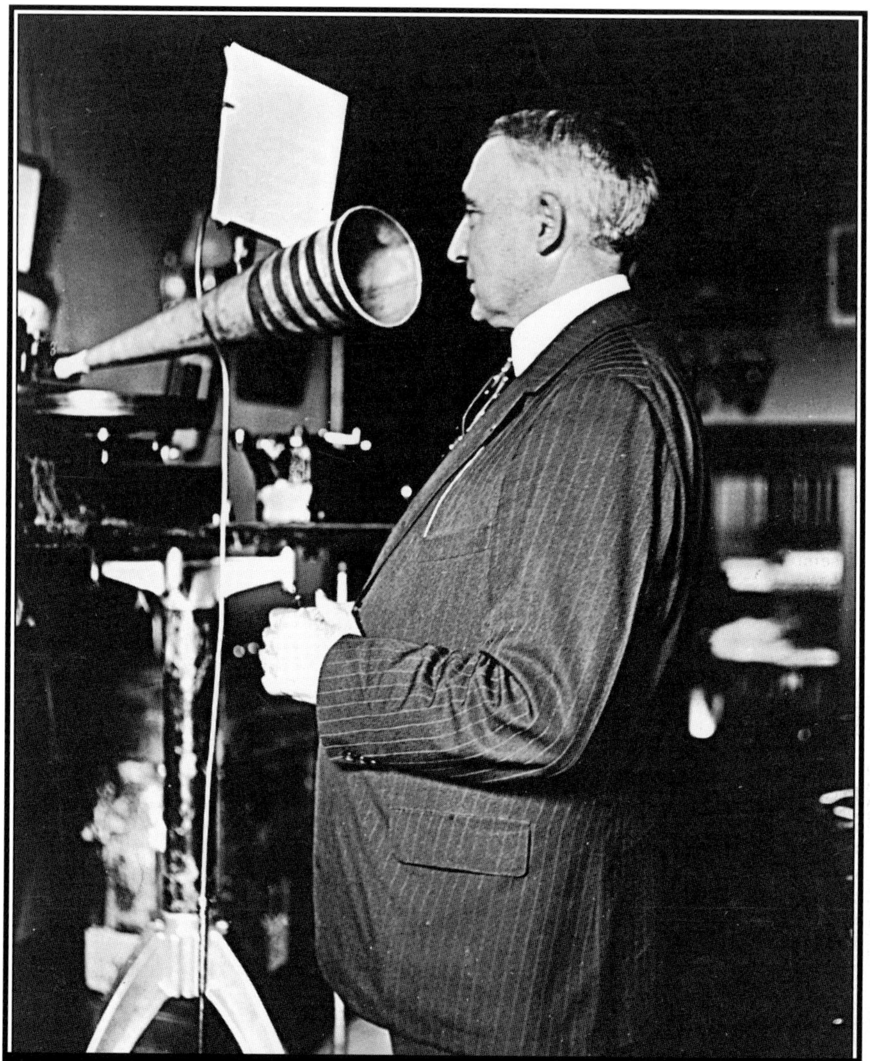

Photo: Library Of Congress

Warren G. Harding records his address "Americanism" on June 29, 1920, for Nation's Forum Records. His recordings, like all of the period, were recorded acoustically, without the benefit of amplification or microphones.

United States will become a member of the League of Nations . . .

We are very much afraid that Colonel Roosevelt would have characterized Mr. Harding's phonograph speech as "weasel words." The aspirations he expressed toward liberty, justice, civilization, and duty are promptly devoured by his declaration that we must hoe our own row, do our duty if we feel like it, but on no account permit any other nation to have a say in the matter, even for counsel. The Chicago platform was in all conscience sufficiently hostile to the League of Nations. Senator Harding's record of votes in the Senate shows him to have been an obedient follower of Senator Lodge in his treaty-wrecking exploits. But we imagine there must be a good many Republicans who will read with astonishment this confession of their candidate's lack of faith in the League of Nations idea.[7]

"Americanism," and the two other Harding recordings here, were recorded for Nation's Forum, a record company established by a St. Louis businessman, Guy Golterman, to enlist support for World War I, and later, to inform Americans of the issues in the presidential campaign of 1920. The Nation's Forum 1920 campaign series would be the last presidential campaign in which the candidates' voices and views were disseminated by a record series. A new, far more pervasive communications medium would soon change political discourse itself.

Enter Radio

Radio has had a close relation to presidential politics almost from the very beginning of its history. It came of age with the Pittsburgh, Pennsylvania, KDKA broadcasts of the Harding-Cox election results of 1920, considered to be the beginning of commercial broadcasting in the United States.[8] More than a million people heard President Harding's June 21, 1923, broadcast speech about the World Court.[9]

Calvin Coolidge

In 1924, radio, covering both Republican and Democratic National Conventions, first broadcast the voices of the presidential candidates.[10] The

President Calvin Coolidge speaking at the amphitheater of Arlington National Cemetery, Memorial Day, 1924.

broadcasts were a huge success. Because radio could capture the immediacy and excitement of a political event, it allowed a speaker to build in emotional pitch. While 78-rpm phonographs had only allowed the campaigners to make five-minute excerpts of their speeches or terse statements of position, radio could carry speeches in their entirety, as well as capture the mood and excitement of the crowd cheering the speech.

Another innovation, electrical recording, also was to make a major difference. Until 1925, the mechanical, acoustical process was used to make records. But the use of electricity overcame most of the acoustic process' limitations, with remarkable results.[11] Electrical recording's tools, microphones and amplifiers, provided wider frequency and dynamic ranges and truer reproduction of sound. On acoustic records, Calvin Coolidge's voice seemed flat and uninteresting, but on the radio:

> An unexpected resonance appeared. The close pickup made necessary by his uninflected delivery emphasized lower tones. Whereas Harding's more traditional oratory had sounded hollow on the air, the Coolidge face-to-face manner proved a revelation, striking in its absence of artifice. Even the nasal quality of his voice seemed to contribute to this. At the same time, the wide-open microphone allowed millions to hear clearly the turning of pages, which seemed to provide a gratifying touch of intimacy.[12]

Coolidge's inaugural address, contained here, is a good example of his effectiveness with a microphone. The effectiveness of radio is also noticeable in several other ways: This is the first speech on this set that is actually a presidential speech, not a campaign speech, and this is the first nearly complete speech presented. (It is *not* complete, because only one master-disc recording machine was used to record the speech. Each time one of the four-minute master-disc blanks was full, a part of the speech was lost while a new master was installed on the machine.)

The preliminary planning for the broadcasting of the inaugural address was carried out by the American Telephone and Telegraph Company, the Radio Corporation of America, and the Chesapeake and Potomac Telephone Company. It was to be broadcast on Inauguration Day, March 4, 1925, and carried by a network of 40 stations linked together by telephone wires, so that Americans throughout the nation could hear the speech. The makeshift network included many of the most famous stations in early broadcasting: WRC in Washington; WJZ and WEAF in New York; WGY, Schenectady; WJAR, Providence; WGR, Buffalo; WCAE, Pittsburgh; WFI, Philadelphia; WDBH, Worcester; WGN, Chicago; KSD, St. Louis; WLW, Cincinnati; WDAF, Kansas City; WOC, Davenport; KGO, Oakland; KOA, Denver; KOW, Portland, Oregon; WOAW, Omaha; KFOA, Seattle; KHJ and KFI, Los Angeles; and KPO, San Francisco.

The broadcast reached an estimated 23 million people. In New York, thousands listened in their homes or crowded before radio and music stores. At President Harding's inauguration, only four years before, he had spoken through a public address system to 125,000 people, and the next day, newspapers had said that "President Harding addressed the greatest number of people that has ever listened to one man's voice at one time in the history of the world." Yet four years later, with the help of radio, *23 million* people heard Coolidge.[13] Radio had arrived.

Philosophically, Calvin Coolidge believed that the least government was the best government:

The Government can do more to remedy the economic ills of the people by a system of rigid economy in public expenditure than can be accomplished through any other action . . . . If the federal government should go out of existence, the common run of people would not detect the difference in the affairs of their daily life for a considerable length of time . . . .The business of America is business.[14]

Coolidge — cool, stable, and utterly incorruptible — was a welcome change from the scandal-ridden Harding administration. In the election of 1924, the front-runner for the Democratic nomination had been Al Smith, a Catholic. At that time, there was a considerable anti-Catholic bias in America, and the Democrats were badly split. After casting 103 ballots, they finally nominated John W. Davis instead. He was little competition for the Republicans, and Coolidge won handily.

President Herbert Hoover (right) is presented with a pressing of his unemployment address by RCA Victor executive Major I. E. Lambert. Victor recorded the 1931 address using its newly developed long-playing record format. The standard five-minute-per-side capacity of a 12-inch 78-rpm disc was nearly tripled by reducing the playing speed to 33⅓-rpm and narrowing the groove width. Victor's 1931 long-playing format was unsuccessful and soon abandoned. The address has not been commercially issued until now.

Herbert Hoover

Hoover had been involved with radio for a long time before he became President. As Secretary of Commerce under Warren G. Harding, he helped frame the first laws regulating the radio industry. He saw its importance early and in 1922 commented on its growth: "We have witnessed, in the last four or five months, one of the most astonishing things that has come under my observation of American life."[15]

It has been stated that Hoover was not particularly effective on the radio, but his speech of October 18, 1931, as the cold, dark Depression winter of 1931-1932 approached, shows that Hoover certainly could make an effective radio speech. It seems that his declining popularity stemmed rather from his philosophy in dealing with the Depression.

Hoover had planned a nationwide fund drive to care for the people who had been thrown out of work, and he was hoping the results of the drive would preclude the appropriation of relief funds by Congress. He had consistently refused to get the federal government involved in combating the Depression, believing that such action was both illegal and morally wrong, and that government intervention was the first step down the road to Socialism or even Communism, which Hoover very deeply feared. Instead, as his speech indicates, he planned a united nationwide drive of state and local community efforts, made up local Community Chests and other organizations to overcome the Depression. The drive was to last five weeks, and every effort was made to ensure its success. In this October 1931 radio speech, Hoover was introduced by Walter Gifford, president of the Chairman's Committee on Unemployment Relief. The program also included music by John Philip Sousa and the United States Marine Band, Lily Pons, and Lawrence Tibbett. One hundred fifty stations carried the broadcast.

Hoover made his speech from Fort Monroe, Virginia, at the entrance to Hampton Roads, en route to Yorktown to address the Yorktown sesquicentennial celebration.[16]

His plea that we must help one another, that "Modern society cannot survive with the defense of Cain, 'Am I my brother's keeper?'" is at the same time eloquent, naive, and sad. His anguish was real, but the Depression would require far more stringent measures than Hoover was willing to take. Hoover's refusal to sanction government intervention angered millions of desperate Americans and made possible Roosevelt's landslide election in 1932.

Franklin D. Roosevelt

Franklin D. Roosevelt was without doubt the President born for radio. As Erik Barnouw relates:

> During 1933 — on March 12, May 7, July 24, October 22 — the new President gave four momentous "fireside chats." These broadcast talks became not only a Franklin D. Roosevelt specialty but milestones in politics and broadcasting. Differing in tone from the broadcasts of Hitler and Mussolini, who were heard in public appearances with a background of hysterical crowds, Roosevelt's "chats" implied a sharing of ideas in a sort of family council. One reflection of their impact was mail response. Until March 1933, one White House employee handled all presidential mail. This arrangement had sufficed even during the 1914-18 World War and the time of panic following the Wall Street crash. But during March 1933, a half million unanswered letters piled up at the White House, and assistants had to be hired.

A portrait of President Franklin D. Roosevelt taken at the time of the broadcast of the First Fireside Chat, March 12, 1933.

Each "chat" swelled the deluge.[17]

The first fireside chat — of March 12, 1933, on President Roosevelt's closing of the banks — is included here. His mastery of the medium is still impressive today, after more than 60 years of radio and television. In 14 minutes, he not only convinces us that the banks are safe, but that it would be unpatriotic to withdraw our funds from them.

On Sunday night, March 12, an estimated sixty million people sat around radio sets to hear the first of President Roosevelt's "fireside chats." In warmly comforting tones, the president assured the nation it was safe now to return their savings to the banks. The next morning, banks opened their doors in the twelve Federal Reserve Bank cities. Nothing so much indicated the sharp shift in public sentiment as the fact that people were now more eager to deposit cash than to withdraw it. "The people trust this administration as they distrusted the other," observed Agnes Meyer. "This is the secret of the whole situation." Since the president had said the banks were safe, they were; Roosevelt, observed Gerald Johnson, "had given a better demonstration than Schopenhauer ever did of the world as Will and Idea." Deprived of cash for several days, people had been expected to withdraw funds to meet immediate needs, yet in every city, deposits far exceeded withdrawals. The crisis was over. "Capitalism," Raymond Moley later concluded, "was saved in eight days."[18]

His windup campaign speech of October 31, 1936, shows Roosevelt in a far different mood. During the summer of 1936, most polls showed Roosevelt the strong winner. Republican strategists, increasingly desperate, decided to attack Roosevelt's Social Security legislation directly. On the weekend before the election, Republican candidate Alf Landon made a strong speech condemning Social Security and stated that the act would lead to the loss of liberty by citizens, since money would be taken from the worker's paycheck compulsorily and might never be returned. Landon's campaign workers then suggested that all workers would have to get mug shots and wear dog tags, so they could be identified. The Hearst newspapers even printed a picture of the alleged dog tag on the day before the election.

The assault, the cynically timed climax of which came so near the campaign's end that effective answer to it was difficult, aroused anxious fears in Democratic campaign headquarters.

It infuriated Franklin Roosevelt.

And on Saturday night, on October 31, in New York City's Madison Square Garden, he struck back in one of the great political speeches in American history.

So eager was he to begin that he became almost angry with the huge crowd before him as it prolonged for a quarter of an hour the ovation that greeted his

President Harry S. Truman delivering his acceptance speech at the Democratic National Convention, Philadelphia, July 15, 1948.

appearance at the lectern. But once he was permitted to begin, he delivered his speech superbly, in wonderfully various, vibrant tones, and with rhythms perfectly suited to the achievement of maximum dramatic effect.[19]

There was some worry that perhaps the language of Roosevelt's speech was too strong, but Roosevelt won the election in a landslide.

Each in different ways, these two speeches display Roosevelt's mastery of the medium. David Halberstam has described Roosevelt's power on the radio and how he personalized the government for many Americans:

> He was the first great American radio voice. For most Americans of this generation, their first memory of politics would be of sitting by a radio and hearing *that* voice, strong, confident, totally at ease. If he was going to speak, the idea of doing something else was unthinkable. If they did not yet have a radio, they walked the requisite several hundred yards to the home of a more fortunate neighbor who did. It was in the most direct sense the government reaching out and touching the citizen, bringing Americans into the political process and focussing their attention as a source of good. Roosevelt was the first professional of the art . . .[20]

Harry Truman and the Election of 1948

Vice President Harry Truman succeeded to the presidency after Roosevelt's death in 1945. By 1948 the polls indicated that Truman had become quite unpopular. Labor was leaving the Democratic Party and instead following the Progressive Party of Henry Wallace. Many of the Southern states, angered by the liberal 1948 civil rights plank in the Democratic platform, formed an independent Dixiecrat movement. After an attempt to draft Dwight D. Eisenhower as a Democratic candidate failed, delegates showed up at the 1948 Democratic convention with signs inscribed: "We're Just Mild About Harry." All polls indicated that Thomas Dewey, the Republican candidate, was the overwhelming favorite.

Part of Truman's problem was his manner of presentation on the radio. J. Leonard Reinsch, his radio advisor, wrote, "From the start, it was clear that Harry Truman had a speaking problem. He spoke much too fast, almost to the point of being unintelligible, with a flat Missouri accent."[21] Alfred Steinberg's *The Man From Missouri* includes a recollection from Charlie Ross, Truman's press secretary, on Truman's turnabout:

> A change came abruptly on April 17 when he spoke to the American Society of Newspaper Editors in Washington. He gave a dull, prepared address, and there was little audience enthusiasm at any point. But when he was off the air, he didn't sit down. Instead, he launched into an extemporaneous, off-the-record talk on national problems from his own point of view. The language was entirely his own, earthy and warm, and the audience went wild. Several editors told Ross later, "If Truman campaigned that way, he'd be a hard guy to beat."[22]

On July 15, 1948, at the Democratic

President Eisenhower poses in his White House office just before starting a farewell television-radio address to the nation, January 17, 1961.

convention in Philadelphia, a new Truman emerged. Truman was not nominated until after midnight, and another hour went by while Alben Barkley, the vice-presidential candidate, was nominated. It was two o'clock in the morning before Truman could speak to a battered, exhausted crowd of delegates.

Instead of reading a set speech, the President spoke from an outline written in short punchy sentences. He expressed his appreciation for the nomination, then his strident, high-pitched tones electrified the audience. "Senator Barkley and I will win this election and make the Republicans like it — don't you forget it!" he declared. "We will do it because they are wrong and we are right . . ."

After enumerating the [80th] Congress' failings, he spoke scornfully of the recent Republican platform, which espoused so many programs rejected by the Congress.

"On the 26th day of July, which out in Missouri we call 'Turnip day,' I am going to call Congress back and ask them to pass laws to halt rising prices, to meet the housing crisis — which they are saying they are for in their platform. At the same time I shall ask them to act upon other vitally needed measures such as aid to education, which they say they are for; a national health program . . . civil rights legislation . . . an increase in the minimum wage . . . Now my friends, if there is any reality behind that Republican platform, we ought to get some action from a short session of the Eightieth Congress. They can do this job in fifteen days, if they want to do it. They will still have time to go out and run for office."

When Truman finished, the delegates rose to their feet and cheered for two minutes. "There was no doubt that he had lifted the delegates out of their doldrums," *Time* reported. "He had roused admiration for his political courage." And for a moment Truman created the illusion — few people regarded it as more than an illusion — that the Democrats had a fighting chance in November.[23]

Although the Republican leaders and Southern Democrats protested this inspired, political maneuver immediately, there was no way for them to get out of the trap that Truman had set for them. Whatever the outcome of the election, the Democrats had given notice that their candidate was a leader and a fighter.

Truman then began a whistle-stop campaign across the country all through the summer of 1948, traveling 21,298 miles and delivering 275 speeches. Reporters began to notice that he was attracting far larger crowds than Dewey and began to wonder if the polls could be wrong. Everyone agreed that, as the campaign went on, Truman was beginning to catch up.

In the election, Truman won by three million votes and received 304 electoral votes. Dewey, totally in shock at the extent of his defeat, said that he felt like the man who awoke inside a coffin with a lily in his hand and said to himself, "If I'm alive, what am I doing here? And if I'm dead, why do I have to go to the bathroom?"

Dwight D. Eisenhower's Farewell Address

During Dwight D. Eisenhower's administration, which coincided with the height of the Cold War (1953-1961), there was an unprecedented growth in federal spending. Eisenhower's farewell speech of January 17, 1961, which warned the American public about the dangers of this spending, was a great surprise and would be one of his most influential speeches. Eisenhower later wrote:

> During the years of my presidency, and especially the later years, I began to feel more and more uneasiness about the effect on the nation of tremendous peacetime military expenditures. In the peaceful life-span of the United States, our practice had been to maintain a minimum defense establishment. We frequently engaged in the rather naive belief that any American could be made into a competent soldier in a matter of weeks or days. Every one of our wars was followed by rapid, drastic demobilization in the assumption that the world had become too civilized to fight again . . .

But Eisenhower, in the wake of the Korean war, decided that this time, the United States would remain strong to deter military aggression. He was already aware of the dangers of this move:

> The makers of the expensive munitions of war, to be sure, like the profits they receive, and the greater the expenditures, the more lucrative the profits. Under the spur of profit potential, powerful lobbies spring up to argue for even larger munitions expenditures. And the web of special interest grows.
>
> Each community in which a manufacturing plant or a military installation is located, profits from the money spent and the jobs created in the area. This fact, of course, constantly presses on the community's political

representatives — congressmen, senators and others — to maintain the facility at maximum strength . . . In the long run, the combinations of pressures for growth can create an almost overpowering influence. Unjustified military spending is nothing more than a distorted use of the nation's resources . . .

The idea, then of making a final address as president to the nation seemed to call on me to warn the nation, again, of the danger in these developments. I could think of no better way to emphasize this than to include a sobering message in what might otherwise have been a farewell of pleasantries.[24]

In October 1951 Eisenhower had written to Charles Wilson, "Any person who doesn't clearly understand that national security and national solvency are mutually dependent, and that permanent maintenance of a crushing weight of military power would eventually produce dictatorship, should not be entrusted with any kind of responsibility in our country."[25] Much has been written about this danger since Dwight Eisenhower's speech, but we should remember that it was Eisenhower — a conservative, a professional soldier, and one of the country's greatest military heroes — who first brought it to our attention.

John F. Kennedy's One Thousand Days

If Franklin D. Roosevelt was made for radio, John F. Kennedy was made for television. Kennedy understood the power and potential of television for a politician, and exploited it. He studied the use of television as a senator and presidential candidate, learning how to appear spontaneous delivering prepared texts and to take advantage of his dashing, youthful appearance.[26]

Kennedy was a master of the spontaneous moment and was the first President to institute live press conferences on television. Perhaps the most famous example of his mastery of television was his first debate with Richard Nixon in 1960. Nixon had been campaigning hard and had lost 20 pounds. He had already given one speech that day. In addition, he had injured his knee and had reinjured it just before the debate. He looked gray and haggard. Kennedy, in contrast, had been campaigning in California, had a tan, and looked relaxed and rested. History has recorded Kennedy as the winner of the debate, not so much on the issues as on his style and appearance. In fact, polls at the time showed that those who heard the debate on the radio favored Nixon; Kennedy won only in the eyes of those who watched the debate on television.

In retrospect, Kennedy did not "win" the debate on looks alone. His aggressive call to get America moving again after eight years of Republican administration immediately put Nixon on the defensive, and Nixon never did quite regain the initiative. Kennedy's powers as a speaker should not be underestimated. He is still probably the most-quoted President since Franklin Roosevelt, and like Roosevelt, he had a gift for rhetoric.

After the Cuban missile crisis and the confrontation with Soviet leader Nikita Khrushchev in the autumn of 1962, President Kennedy tried to reach an understanding with the Russians. He particularly wanted a ban on atmospheric nuclear testing. Kennedy sent Averill Harriman to Moscow to talk to Khrushchev directly and himself delivered a speech on the subject of the Cold War and nuclear testing. The speech, one of Kennedy's best, was given on June 10, 1963, at the commencement ceremonies at American University in Washington, D.C. Theodore Sorensen, presidential speechwriter, later wrote:

I obtained material from [Norman] Cousins, [McGeorge] Bundy, [Carl] Kaysen, my brother Tom, and others, and gathered appropriate passages that had been cut from the inaugural address in 1961, or discarded when the Kennedy-Khrushchev TV exchange fell through in 1962, or used in previous Kennedy speeches and worthy of repetition. Unlike most foreign policy speeches — none of which turned out to be so sweeping in concept and impact as this turned out to be — official departmental positions and suggestions were not solicited. The president was determined to put forward a fundamentally new emphasis on the peaceful and the positive in our relations with the Soviets. He did not want that new policy diluted by the usual threats of destruction, boasts of nuclear stockpiles, and lectures on Soviet treachery.[27]

Arthur Schlesinger called the speech "affirmative in tone, elevated in language, wise and subtle in analysis. Its central substantive proposal was a moratorium on atmospheric testing; but its effect was to redefine the whole national attitude toward the Cold War. It was a brilliant and faithful reproduction of the President's views, and we read it with mounting admiration and excitement."[28] Khrushchev called it "the greatest speech by any American President since Roosevelt" and offered a limited ban on atmospheric testing and testing in space and underwater. Perhaps more significantly, he said that only madmen could hope to destroy capitalism by nuclear war.

Kennedy's American University speech was a monumental one. When he checked his mail, he found that the speech had provoked 896 letters, most favorable. In the same period, 28,232 people had sent letters about a freight rate bill. "The President, tossing the report aside, said with disgust, 'That is why I tell people in Congress that they're crazy if they take their mail seriously.'"[29]

John F. Kennedy as he appeared on television in 1960 during a presidential debate with Republican candidate Richard Nixon.

Photo: Cecil Stoughton, LBJ Library Collection

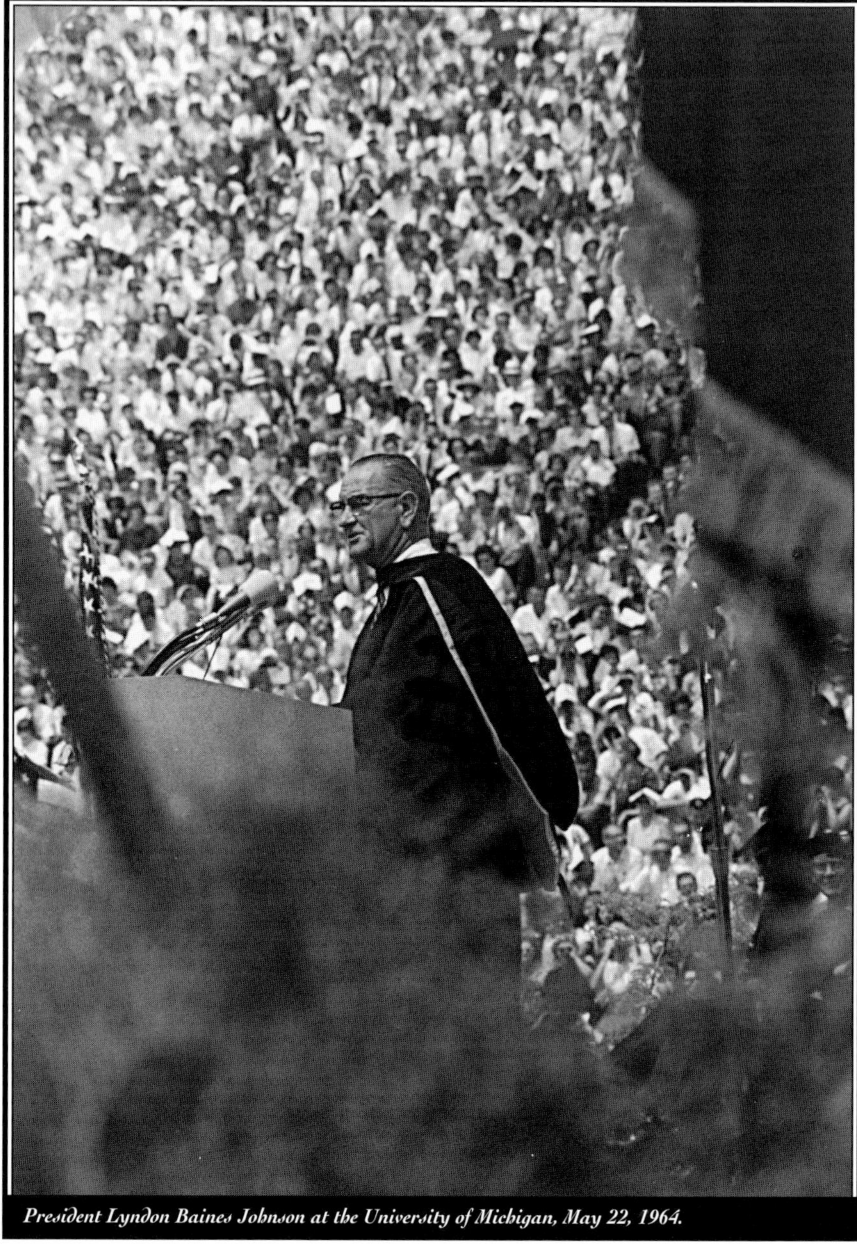

President Lyndon Baines Johnson at the University of Michigan, May 22, 1964.

Lyndon Baines Johnson

Vice President Lyndon B. Johnson ascended to the presidency on November 22, 1963, following the assassination of John F. Kennedy. Johnson, the former Senate Leader from Texas and an expert and experienced politician, continued the Democratic tradition of an active, interventionist federal government. In his speech of May 22, 1964, President Johnson introduced the concept of the Great Society. From Merle Miller's *Lyndon: An Oral Biography*:

> As Lyndon's interim presidency neared its halfway mark and the elections loomed ahead, he became progressively concerned with finding his own hallmark, some phrase that would encompass his aims the way Roosevelt's

New Deal, Truman's Fair Deal, and Kennedy's New Frontier had encompassed theirs. Some phrase that would catch on with the press, the people, the historians . . .

Moyers suggested that [Dick] Goodwin might try to formulate such a speech as the president was looking for . . .

It is generally agreed that the term Great Society as a Johnson label was conceived that night when Goodwin sat down at his typewriter to hammer out the memorial speech . . .

Jack Valenti: "Goodwin was pleased with the [Great Society] speech, a jewel of a speech. The president was pleased with it; he felt that it told in clear and sometimes ringing tones what he felt was the direction he wanted to take this country."[30]

Johnson gave the speech on a hot, sunny day in Ann Arbor before almost 5,000 people.

Charles Roberts: "The day I rode back from Ann Arbor to Washington in his plane — that was what I would call the president in his manic phase. I don't use that term critically. I just mean he was absolutely euphoric.

"He was popular then. Dick Goodwin had written him a hell of a speech, and he delivered it well. The crowd seemed to get the idea that he was laying out a new program, that this was the new Johnson program coming on . . .

"That was the unveiling of the Great Society, his own program, the program he was going to run on the next fall.

"He was a compulsive talker mostly when he was in this buoyant, euphoric mood after giving a speech or when things were going right for him. And of course during all that great first year that he was so euphoric, the Vietnam thing was still just a cloud no bigger than a man's hand."[31]

Some of the programs of the Great Society were: Medicare, Medicaid, Head Start, the Job Corps, community action grants, Foster Grandparents, Upward Bound, community health centers, legal services for the poor, Vista, and college work-study programs.[32]

Richard Nixon

In 1968 American involvement in the Vietnam War brutally divided the nation's conscience. The Democratic Party especially was torn by the war, and at the Democratic convention in Chicago in 1968, rioting broke out between pro-war and anti-war factions. As a result, while the Democrats were hopelessly divided, Republican Richard Nixon won the presidency in 1968.

Republican victory did not end the bitter controversy in the United States about the Vietnam War. Demonstrations against the war intensified. Against this backdrop Richard Nixon made his "Silent Majority" speech of November 3, 1969. Nixon later wrote:

In October 1969, hundreds of thousands of anti-Vietnam War demonstrators marched into Washington. They demonstrated, sometimes violently, around the White

House and the Capitol and the downtown area. Peace-at-any-price senators and congressmen demanded that I withdraw American forces from Vietnam in return for our prisoners of war. Even some of my own political friends joined the pack. They contended that since Kennedy and Johnson had sent combat troops to Vietnam, I would gain politically by bringing them home, regardless of the impact on foreign policy. I was inundated with conflicting advice from the Cabinet, my staff, and members of Congress.

I scheduled a television speech for November 3. I knew that it would be the most important speech of my presidency so far. I also knew that the conclusion of the speech would determine whether it would be a success or failure. At 2:00 a.m. the night before the speech, as I sat alone in the study at Camp David, an idea came to me. I wrote it by hand into the text. It read: "I have chosen a plan for peace. I believe it will succeed. If it does succeed, what the critics say now won't matter. If it does not succeed, anything I say now won't matter. And so tonight — to you, the great silent majority of my fellow Americans, I ask for your support. Let us be united for peace. Let us also be united against defeat. Because let us understand: North Vietnam cannot defeat or humiliate the United States. Only Americans can do that...."

The reaction by telegram, letters, and telephone was the biggest ever. My approval rating went up eleven points, the biggest increase as a result of a presidential speech in the history of the Gallup poll....

President Richard Nixon in Washington D.C., February 1969.

Chief Justice Warren E. Burger (right) administers the presidential oath of office to Gerald Ford while Mrs. Ford looks on, August 9, 1974.

The "Silent Majority" speech met the test. Any doubts I may have had about it were removed when dovish senators and congressmen who had urged me to order a withdrawal of American troops began to wear American flags on their lapels. The silent majority in the country had finally spoken, created a new majority in the Congress, and given our Vietnam policies a chance to succeed.[33]

But the speech is significant for far more than its application to the war in Vietnam. Nixon may have won in 1968 because of deep divisions in the Democratic Party, but the favorable response to the speech, especially to the idea of a "silent majority," and his subsequent victory in the 1972 election, suggested a major realignment of the voters. The new, pro-Republican majority consisted of middle-class voters, especially in the West and the South, who were deeply disturbed by the changes that were taking place within American society and who also were fed up with an increasingly intrusive federal government. This new Republican majority would dominate presidential American politics from 1980 to 1992.

William Safire later wrote:

> In retrospect, the "silent majority" speech was the most important of his first term, not so much for what the president said but for what the speech did. A bona fide event, a studied counterpunch to the events staged by a minority bidding to become dominant, the speech moved the country in the direction the president wanted it moved and most of the country wanted to be moved.[34]

Gerald Ford

President Ford's address of August 9, 1974, is the first inaugural address on this disc since that of Calvin Coolidge in 1925, but the circumstances could not have been more different.

For more than two years, the Watergate scandal had deeply divided the nation. Ultimately, the unfolding of the scandal had paralyzed the presidency of Richard Nixon. On August 9, 1974, facing impeachment proceedings stemming from Watergate, the President resigned. Shortly after 9:30 a.m., Richard Nixon and his wife left the White House by helicopter.

> They swept out of the door, followed by the Fords, down the red carpet and into the chopper. The crewmen stood at stiff salute. Nixon flashed the "V" for victory signal of a thousand campaign send-offs — I don't recall noting the irony of it. The rotors accelerated. The shrubbery and the trees of the White House shook and swayed as in a summer storm. We turned our faces from the blast. Then we turned back for a final wave, and it was over.[35]

At 11:45, Gerald Ford left the vice-presidential office for the Red Room of the White House, where he was sworn in by Chief Justice Warren Burger. After taking the oath of office, President Ford made the short, extremely moving speech that is heard here. His remarks express both his grief for Richard Nixon, his associate and close friend for 25 years, and his need for help from his fellow Americans as he shouldered the awesome responsibility of the presidency. Gerald Ford's speech was an important first step in healing the wounds left by Watergate.

James Earl (Jimmy) Carter

In the aftermath of Vietnam and Watergate, the American people, disillusioned, elected a Democratic "outsider," Georgian Jimmy Carter, to the White House. Carter drew his strength from grass roots America, but he never found an effective power base in Washington.

By the summer of 1979, America seemed to be in deep trouble. Inflation was worsening steadily, while the economy remained dormant. Iranians had taken Americans hostage, and the nation appeared powerless to do anything about it.

But perhaps most symptomatic of America's anger and frustration were the fuel shortages. All over the United States, there were long lines of cars waiting for gasoline. As engines overheated and tempers frayed, motorists cursed Middle East oil suppliers, the federal government, and sometimes the technology that had made us its prisoners. Americans had probably not felt so impotent since the Depression.

Against this backdrop, President Carter presented his "Energy Address" of July 15, 1979. It was only partly on energy. In seclusion at Camp David, Carter had invited open discussion among various members of the government and his own cabinet to elicit their perceptions of what was wrong with the country. He received frank, often critical answers. His speech, incorporating these criticisms, was much more an address on the people's lack of confidence in the nation than a speech on energy.

> That Sunday night, July 15, 1979, I tried to express to the American people what I had learned at Camp David. I spoke from the Oval Office about the need to have faith in our country — not only in the government, but in our own ability to solve great problems. There was a growing disrespect in our churches, schools, news media, and other institutions; this change had not come suddenly or without cause.
>
> I acknowledged that we had some serious problems, but expressed my

confidence that we could solve them if we were willing to work together with courage and concern for one another.

I pointed out that we had lost confidence in our government but that it was time for us to work together to realize the potential greatness of America and to solve the energy problem as a major test. Everyone could help. I quoted one of the visitors to Camp David: "We've got to stop crying and start sweating, stop talking and start walking, stop cursing and start praying. The strength we need will not come from the White House, but from every house in America."

I closed with a brief outline of the new energy proposals, which would be described more completely the next day. It was one of my best speeches, and the response to it was overwhelmingly positive. Intrigued by the mystery of what I would say, about one hundred million people had listened — perhaps the largest American audience I ever had.[36]

The speech, later known as Carter's "Malaise Speech," became highly controversial. But the crisis of confidence was all too real, and Carter deserves our admiration for pointing it out and trying to deal with it in the open. Unfortunately for him, it was probably this crisis that caused the Reagan landslide victory in 1980.

Ronald Reagan

Like John F. Kennedy, Ronald Reagan was a natural for television. He was good-looking, with a winning smile, and his years of training in motion pictures and television taught him poise and a natural presence that convinced audiences he was addressing them in particular. And like Kennedy, he understood that style counts on television. Reagan told T. H. White that there were two very important moments in his 1980 campaign. First, in Nashua, New Hampshire, Reagan was to

President Jimmy Carter preparing for his address on energy from the Oval Office of the White House, July 15, 1979.

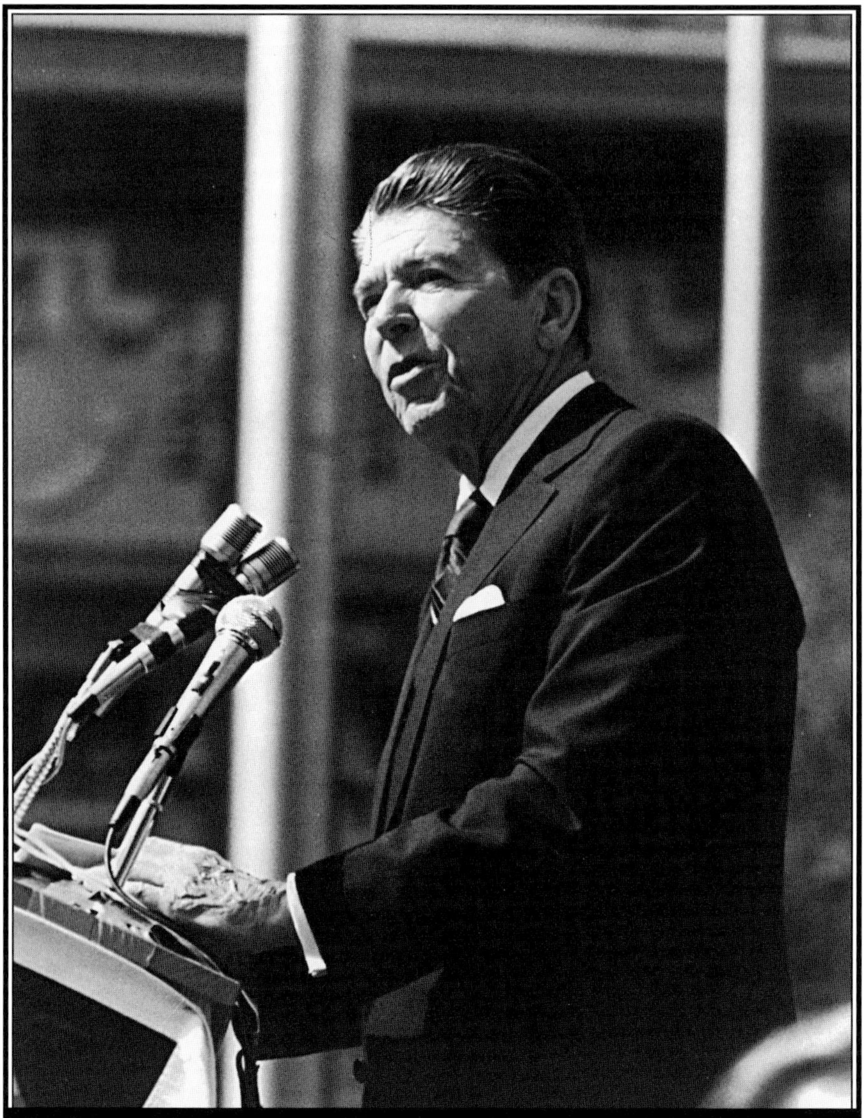

Photo: Library Of Congress

President Ronald Reagan, 1981.

debate George Bush at the Nashua High School. But Reagan decided to change the rules and ask all the Republican candidates to debate without discussing the change in format with Bush. John Breen, the executive editor of the Nashua *Telegraph* and moderator, was furious.

What follows could not have been more than ninety seconds of drama. Ronald Reagan reaches for the microphone to explain the tableau. Mr. Breen snaps aloud to the technicians: "Turn Mr. Reagan's microphone off." Then Reagan jackknifes up from his chair, grabs the microphone in a single swoop, his temper flaring, and yells, "I paid for this show. I'm paying for this microphone, Mr. Green [sic]."

The swoop, the grace, the perfect flow of the dramatic gesture, could not have been better if rehearsed a dozen times.

Here was an indignant citizen defending his rights; the outraged citizen taking no lip from a motorcycle cop; the workingman talking back to management . . .[37]

The second, more famous moment took place during the Reagan-Carter debate when, after Carter had attacked Reagan's record on Medicare, Reagan shook his head ruefully and said to Carter, "There you go again." In both instances, Reagan came across as a man in complete charge, a man who could exert forceful leadership. To a nation that felt helpless, these moments were crucial in Reagan's successful election campaign.

On May 31, 1988, at Moscow University, beneath a huge bust of Lenin, Ronald Reagan gave a speech before 600 of Mikhail Gorbachev's Soviet elite. As he did so often in the United States, Reagan captivated his audience.

It was the third day of President Reagan's trip to the Soviet Union, and the trip had not been an unqualified success. Gorbachev had visited the United States the previous December, and it looked as if there might be a real thaw in the Cold War, which had been going on since 1945. President Reagan's insistence on talking about human rights had apparently irritated Gorbachev. But Reagan endeared himself to his Soviet audience with this speech, and *The New York Times* devoted a glowing editorial to Reagan's performance:

With Lenin Watching
It may have been Ronald Reagan's finest oratorical hour. For *this* president especially, the setting alone was stunning — an audience of students at Mikhail Gorbachev's own alma mater, beneath a huge bust of Lenin, in front of a mural of the Russian Revolution. And the speech Mr. Reagan made on that stage yesterday was equally remarkable, a tribute to the maturing of his own views, to the daring of Mikhail Gorbachev's reforms and to the normalizing of American-Soviet relations . . . .

The speech extended the president's persistent, laudable expressions of concern for human rights this week — often to Soviet displeasure. A Soviet commentator said critically that it was as if Mr. Gorbachev in Washington last December had met with homeless people, American Indians and others who are disaffected. It was an incomplete parallel. If Mr. Gorbachev wished to have such meetings, why didn't he? A president emphasizes human rights not because Americans are perfect but because they care about human rights.

If the U.S. emphasis was appropriate, the Soviet displeasure was to be expected. The two nations can aim at a relationship in which differences can be dealt with forthrightly. The two leaders seem to be able to move readily between moments of criticism to substantive work and good spirits . . . .

How did the president who called the Soviet Union an evil empire come to this thoughtful balance of sentiments? Walking in Red Square with Mr. Gorbachev, he gave an answer. "What we have decided to do is talk to each other rather than about each other, and it's working just fine." When people some day look back to the milestones of the Cold War, they are likely to remember the day Ronald Reagan extolled freedom, while Lenin looked on.[38]

George Bush

The last two speeches on this set, selected by Presidents who gave them, provide the listener with a paradigm of America's attempt to deal with international and domestic problems. President Bush's speech deals with America's role abroad, President Clinton's with its role at home.

President Bush's greatest successes were in the international arena; he was keenly interested in foreign policy. Much of his prepresidential experience was in foreign affairs. As President, he showed great flexibility and sensitivity to changing international situations, as is clearly demonstrated by the speech presented here.

President Bush traveled extensively in Europe in the summer of 1989, and while there he made a series of speeches. The speech on this set was delivered at Leiden in the Netherlands on July 17, 1989. In it, President Bush called for a new alignment of nations in NATO, and a strengthening of the European powers. The *New York Times* noted in the speech a shift in emphasis in the President's policy:

With the European agenda shifting rapidly away from military issues and toward economic ones, President Bush has over the last three months defined a more modest role for the United States on this side of the Atlantic: merely first among equals.

In Brussels in May and again two days ago in the Netherlands, Mr. Bush startled and delighted the Allies by voicing unequivocal support for Western European economic and military integration that in the long run implies a certain American disengagement from the continent.

In a speech from the Dutch city of Leiden on Monday, Mr. Bush

"To keep the peace in Europe is to keep the peace for America." President George Bush addresses the residents of Leiden, the Netherlands, July 17, 1989.

declared: "Let me say clearly a stronger Europe, a more united Europe is good for my country; it's good for the United States of America. And it's a development we welcome, a natural evolution within our alliance, the product of true partnership 40 years in the making."[39]

So much has happened since July 1989 that this speech seems almost to belong to another era. New questions have emerged about NATO's role in the new Europe, and America's role within NATO.

With the fall of the Iron Curtain, the subsequent fragmentation of the Soviet Union, the reemergence of a virulent nationalism in the Balkans, and the rise of a militant, fundamentalist Islam, new international tensions have quickly replaced the old. The United Nations and NATO often seem unable to cope with these new international conflicts. The United States coordinated the Persian Gulf War after Iraq invaded Kuwait, but the United States and other United Nations members have been unable to gain any political advantage from their stunning military victory. The hopeful note Bush's speech sounded seems to have faded away.

Bill Clinton

In 1992 Bill Clinton defeated George Bush to be elected the first Democratic President since Jimmy Carter in 1976.

In the wake of the end of the Cold War, Clinton's victory seemed to signal a shift of the voters to a more liberal mood. But the mood in 1992 was very different from that in 1932. Like Hoover in 1932, George Bush may have lost in 1992 because his party seemed unable to cope with the country's domestic problems. But more important, the vote for Mr. Clinton seemed to represent a dissatisfaction with all incumbent politicians, rather than a wish for any great change in ideology.

It has sometimes been said that Clinton is not a great orator. But if evidence is needed of President Clinton's ability to stir our emotions and to inspire us, one needs only to hear his eloquent speech to the Convocation of the Mason Temple Church of God in Christ in Memphis. At this church, Martin Luther King Jr. gave his final sermon, on April 3, 1968, the day before he was assassinated.

President Clinton's speech, delivered on November 13, 1993, was not listed as a major address, and media attention was focused on the North American Free Trade Agreement. But perhaps because he was inspired by his surroundings, Clinton gave perhaps his most moving speech to date, expressing his deep anguish at the United States tearing itself apart. He predicted what Martin Luther King Jr. would say to us if he returned to America today:

> But he would say, I did not live and die to see the American family destroyed. I did not live and die to see 13-year-old boys get automatic weapons and gun down 9-year-olds just for the kick of it. I did not live and die to see young people destroy their own lives with drugs and then build fortunes destroying the lives of others. That is not what I came here to do.

E. J. Dionne in the *Washington Post* said of this speech:

> Clinton's single most successful speech as president was his address to a convention of black ministers in Memphis. He spoke movingly about racism and also about personal responsibility, family breakup, and the moral costs of unemployment and crime. He argued that government had a role to play in solving problems, but that only

President William J. Clinton delivering his address to the Convocation of the Church of God in Christ in Memphis, Tennessee, November 13, 1993.

individuals and communities could solve the country's moral crisis. Instead of looking slippery, he looked gutsy. And he did so while saying things that most Americans felt they needed to hear . . . .[40]

George Bush presents his vision of a new world order in which a united Europe comes into its own, somewhat disengaged from the United States. Bill Clinton presents his vision of an America where the federal government helps its citizens, but where individuals most ultimately solve their deepest problems. Both speeches are optimistic, but both suggest that Americans are still undecided about what government can accomplish — both abroad and at home — and what it cannot.

In different ways, all of the speeches on this set addressed these questions. As the 20th century draws to an end, it appears that there is no one answer. Rather, as Arthur Schlesinger has suggested, Americans go in cycles, voting first for a President who pledges an interventionist style at home and abroad, then for one who promises to reduce the role of government in our lives. These speeches show how arguments on one side or another have played in differing political contexts, and serve as an excellent framework for understanding America's continuing, essential debate.

—*Cooper C. Graham*

Cooper C. Graham is a graduate of the Law School of the University of Virginia and received his Ph.D. in Cinema Studies from New York University in 1984. He is the coauthor of D. W. Griffith And The Biograph Company *(1984), author of* Leni Riefenstahl And Olympia *(1986), and has also compiled several finding aids for the Library of Congress's recorded sound collections dealing with World War II. Dr. Graham is currently acquisitions specialist for the Motion Picture, Broadcasting and Recorded Sound Division of the Library of Congress.*

1. Cabell Phillips, "Torchlight, Train, Television," *New York Times*, September 8, 1960.
2. "Edison Records by Wm. H. Taft," *Talking Machine World*, August 15, 1908, p. 35.
3. "Bryan Ridicules Taft Imitations," *Richmond Times Dispatch*, August 5, 1908, p. 8.
4. "Campaign Duel Fought in Spokane," *The Spokesman-Review*, September 27, 1908, part V, p. 1.
5. "Roosevelt in Emporia," *Emporia Gazette*, September 23, 1912, p. 1.

6. U. S. Senate, Committee on Privileges and Elections. *Campaign Contributions. Testimony Before A Subcommittee Of The Committee On Privileges And Elections United States Senate. Sixty Second Congress Third Session.* Vol. 1, p. 133.; Austin Leigh Moore, *John Archbold And The Early Development Of Standard Oil* (New York: Columbia University, 193-), p. 270.

7. *New York Times*, July 1, 1920, p. 12.

8. Erik Barnouw, *A History Of Broadcasting In The United States* (New York: Oxford University Press, 1966), Vol. 1, pp. 71-2; Orrin E. Dunlap, Jr., "How It All Started." *New York Times*, November 1, 1936.

9. Erik Barnouw, *op. cit.*, p. 146.

10. Cabell Phillips, *op. cit.*

11. Oliver Read, *The Recording And Reproduction Of Sound* (Indianapolis: Howard W. Sams & Co., Inc. 1952), pp. 14-17.

12. Erik Barnouw, *op. cit.*, p. 146, citing Archer, *History Of Radio: To 1926* (New York: American Historical Company, 1938), p. 324.

13. "Entire Nation Will Hear Inaugural Ceremony By Radio," *New York Times*, January 25, 1925, VIII, p. 13: "22,800,000 Listened to Coolidge On Radio," *New York Times*, March 5, 1925, p. 6.

14. Frank Freidel, *America In The Twentieth Century* (New York; Alfred A. Knopf, 1964), pp. 243-44.

15. Barnouw, *op. cit.*, p. 4.

16. "Herbert Hoover Opens Drive For Community And For The Nation's Idle," *The New York Times*, October 19, 1931, pp. 1, 4.

17. Erik Barnouw, *op. cit.*, Vol. 2, p. 7.

18. William E. Leuchtenberg, *Franklin D. Roosevelt And The New Deal 1932-1940* (New York: Harper & Row, 1962), pp. 44-45.

19. Kenneth S. Davis, *FDR: The New Deal Years* (New York: Random House, 1986), p. 644.

20. David Halberstam, *The Powers That Be* (New York; Alfred A. Knopf, 1979), pp. 14-17.

21. J. Leonard Reinsch, *Getting Elected* (New York: Hippocrene Books, 1988), p. 12.

22. Alfred Steinberg, *The Man From Missouri* (New York: G.P. Putnam's Sons, 1962), p. 311.

23. Irwin Ross, *The Loneliest Campaign* (New York: New American Library, 1968), pp. 129-130.

24. Dwight D. Eisenhower, *The White House Years: Waging The Peace, 1959-1961* (New York: Doubleday & Co., 1965), pp. 614-15.

25. Blanche Wiesen Cook, *The Declassified Eisenhower* (New York: Doubleday & Co., 1981), p. 345.

26. Halberstam, *op. cit.*, pp. 324-25.

27. Theodore C. Sorensen, *Kennedy* (New York: Harper and Row, 1965), pp. 730-31.

28. Arthur M. Schlesinger, *A Thousand Days; John F. Kennedy In The White House* (New York: Greenwich House, 1983), p. 900.

29. Schlesinger, *op. cit.*, p. 910.

30. Merle Miller, *Lyndon: An Oral Biography* (New York: G.P. Putnam's Sons, 1980), pp.375-76.

31. Miller, *op. cit.*, pp. 376-77.

32. Tom Wicker, "L.B.J.'s Great Society," *The New York Times*, May 7, 1990, p. A17.

33. Richard Nixon, *In The Arena* (New York: Simon and Schuster, 1990), pp. 215-216.

34. William Safire, *After the Fall* (Garden City, New York: Doubleday & Company, 1975), pp. 177-78.

35. Robert T. Hartmann, *Palace Politics* (New York: McGraw-Hill, 1980), p. 170.

36. Jimmy Carter, *Keeping Faith* (New York: Bantam Books, 1982), pp. 120-121.

37. T. H. White, *The Making Of The President 1956-1980* (Norwalk, Connecticut: The Eaton Press, 1982), p. 31.

38. *New York Times*, July 1, 1988, p. A30.

39. James M. Markham, "For Europe, A New Look," *New York Times*, July 20, 1989, p. A9.

40. E. J. Dionne, Jr., "Lost Threads Of A Presidency," *Washington Post*, August 2, 1994, p. A15.

The White House, sometime around the turn of the century.

This set of recordings is the first to be issued in a series of collaborations between Rhino Records and the Library of Congress. The Library holds the nation's largest public collection of sound recordings and radio — nearly three million items. Its Motion Picture, Broadcasting and Recorded Sound Division is responsible for the acquisition, preservation, and reference service for these recordings. The division is also responsible for the Library's extensive film and television collections.

The Library of Congress acquired its first sound recording in 1904: a wax cylinder recording of the voice of Kaiser Wilhelm II of Germany. It began to systematically collect recordings in 1925 when the Victor Talking Machine Company, in the interest of archival preservation, gave the Library a selection of its phonograph records. Rival companies followed its example. Because there was no federal copyright law for sound recordings, and no corollary deposit requirement for sound recordings until 1972, the Library's initial collection was developed almost solely through gifts from individuals and corporations. Private collectors have donated thousands of recorded treasures; performing artists have contributed copies of their radio programs, and corporations and associations have transferred their recorded archives to the nation. The collections continue to benefit from the generosity of donors. Recently, more than 100,000 jazz and popular music 78-rpm discs were donated to the Library by a private collector.

The Library of Congress sound recording collection now represents more than 100 years of recording, reflecting the entire spectrum of recorded sound from wax cylinders to digital audio tapes. Particular subject strengths are spoken-word recordings, chamber music, opera, and American music of all types: jazz, rock, folk, musical theater, popular, and classical.

The holdings also reflect a century of American life and culture and include a number of collections of unusual historical interest. Major broadcasting and other spoken-word sound collections include NBC Radio, Armed Forces Radio and Television Service, Office of War Information (World War II propaganda), British Broadcasting Corporation Sound Archive, and the Archive of Poetry and Literature on Tape.

The audio collections of the Library have proven to be an invaluable resource for musicians, scholars, and production companies in need of historic musical and documentary sound recordings. Very often, record companies draw on the unparalleled archival holdings of the Library for reissue materials. In order to assure that these collections are preserved for posterity, the Library is not able to play back its sound recordings for purely personal purposes. The collaboration with Rhino, and this publication of Presidents' speeches, represents a significant effort by the Library to share its treasures more widely with the public.

For further information about the Library's sound and moving image collections or services, write to the Motion Picture, Broadcasting and Recorded Sound Division, Library of Congress, Washington, D.C. 20540-4800.

Landmarks in the Presidents' Administrations

William Howard Taft, 1909-1913

1909
Robert Peary reaches North Pole; Frederick A. Cook claims to have preceded him by a year
National Association for the Advancement of Colored People (NAACP) organized
1910
Union of South Africa formed
Congress establishes a seniority system in reaction to the power of Speaker Joe Cannon
Paul Ehrlich creates first antibacterial drug to treat victims of syphilis
1911
Standard Oil Co. dissolved by order of the U.S. Supreme Court
Roald Amundsen and party reach South Pole
Woodrow Wilson becomes governor of New Jersey
Ronald Reagan born
1912
New Mexico becomes the 47th state
Arizona becomes the 48th state
R.M.S. Titanic hits an iceberg and sinks, killing more than 1,500 passengers
Theodore Roosevelt bolts the Republican Party and runs for President on the Progressive or "Bull Moose" ticket

Theodore Roosevelt, 1901-1909

1901
William McKinley assassinated; Theodore Roosevelt becomes President
Texas oil industry established with Spindletop oil well
Queen Victoria dies
U.S. Steel Co. founded
William Howard Taft becomes governor of the Philippines
1902
Bureau of the Census established
Reclamation Act passed by Congress
Cuba established as independent republic
1903
Wright brothers fly
Hepburn law regulates railroad rates
Pacific Ocean cable opened
1904
Panama Canal begun
Russo-Japanese War begins in Manchuria
First installment finance company organized in Rochester, New York
1905
Russian revolution begins with Winter Palace massacre
Pogroms begin in Russia
Roosevelt mediates end of Russo-Japanese War; becomes only President to receive Nobel Peace Prize
Albert Einstein publishes *Special Theory of Relativity*
1906
San Francisco earthquake and fires
Pure Food and Drug Act enacted

William Howard Taft appointed Provisional Governor of Cuba
1907
Financial panic
Oklahoma made 46th state
1908
First Ford Model T made
FBI created
General Motors organized
Lyndon B. Johnson born

Woodrow Wilson, 1913-1921
1913
16th Amendment to the Constitution ratified: Authorizes income tax
17th Amendment ratified: Permits direct election of U.S. senators
Henry Ford introduces the assembly line to his automobile plant
Richard Nixon born
Gerald Ford born
1914
World War I starts
Panama Canal opens
1915
S.S. *Lusitania* sunk by a German submarine
Ku Klux Klan revived to guarantee white supremacy
Warren Harding becomes U.S. senator from Ohio
Dwight D. Eisenhower graduates from West Point
1916
Gen. John Pershing sent to Mexico to capture Pancho Villa
Albert Einstein publishes *General Theory of Relativity*
Irish Easter rebellion
National Park Service created
1917
U.S. declares war against Germany
Romanov dynasty ends in Russia
Bolshevik revolution begins; Vladimir Ilyich Lenin heads new government
British issue Balfour Declaration
Herbert Hoover appointed U.S. Food Administrator
Harry S. Truman is an Army 1st Lieutenant in France
John F. Kennedy born
1918
Flu epidemic kills more than 21 million people
Russia withdraws from World War I
Wilson announces Fourteen Points
World War I ends; 10 million dead, 20 million disabled
1919
Versailles Peace Treaty conference begins; U.S. Senate will reject treaty and membership in the League of Nations
Russian civil war pits Bolshevik Red Army forces against White Russian Army
18th Amendment: Prohibits manufacture and sale of alcoholic beverages
Theodore Roosevelt dies
1920
19th Amendment: Women given right to vote

Prohibition goes into effect
Nicola Sacco and Bartolomeo Vanzetti are arrested for killing a factory guard during a robbery in Massachusetts
Franklin D. Roosevelt unsuccessfully runs for Vice President

Warren Harding, 1921-1923
1921
Persia expels Russian army in a bloodless coup
Widespread strikes by U.S. workers in response to cut wages
Emergency Quota Act establishes immigration limits by nationality
First of many Russian concentration camps established by Lenin
William Howard Taft becomes Chief Justice of the United States
Herbert Hoover becomes Secretary of Commerce
1922
Naval Disarmament Conference treaty sets naval limitations on U.S., Britain, Japan, France, and Italy
Benito Mussolini granted dictatorial powers in Italy

Calvin Coolidge, 1923-1929
1923
Warren Harding dies; Calvin Coolidge succeeds
U.S.S.R. formally created
Adolf Hitler and the National Socialist German Workers party make an unsuccessful effort to overthrow the Bavarian government (the "Beer Hall Putsch")
1924
Lenin dies; Josef Stalin begins to consolidate power
Johnson-Reed Immigration Act sets stricter immigration quotas
Jimmy Carter born
George Bush born
1925
Hitler's *Mein Kampf* published
Brotherhood of Sleeping Car Porters founded by A. Philip Randolph
Bell Laboratories is established by AT&T

President Calvin Coolidge and Vice President Charles G. Dawes review their inaugural parade, March 4, 1925.

John Scopes trial challenges teaching of evolution theory
1926
Stalin established as dictator of Soviet Union
U.S. troops land in Nicaragua to restore order during a revolt and to protect U.S. businesses
Robert Goddard launches first liquid-fuel rocket
1927
Charles Lindbergh makes the first solo nonstop flight across the Atlantic Ocean
Despite legal and social protests, convicted murderers Sacco and Vanzetti are electrocuted
1928
Antibiotic power of penicillin discovered
Chiang Kai-shek is elected president of China
First Soviet Five-Year Plan established by Stalin
Franklin D. Roosevelt elected governor of New York

Herbert Hoover, 1929-1933
1929
October stock market crash; $30 billion in capital disappears
1930
Stock prices continue to decline
U.S. unemployment reaches 4 million
1,300 banks close since crash
Hawley-Smoot Act raises tariffs
Civil disobedience against Britain in India begun by Mahatma Gandhi
U.S. South and Midwest suffer severe drought
Radio set sales: 13.5 million
Radio advertising: $60 million
1931
Unemployment climbs over 8 million
2,294 banks fail
1932
Bonus Army driven from Washington D.C. by Gen. Douglas MacArthur
Unemployment over 15 million
Route 66, from Chicago to Los Angeles, opens
Charles Lindbergh Jr. is kidnapped and later found murdered

Franklin D. Roosevelt, 1933-1945
1933
Bank holiday ordered
National Labor Board established
20th Amendment: Congressional terms of office and inauguration date changed
21st Amendment: Prohibition ends
16 million unemployed
Hitler made chancellor of Germany
Civilian Conservation Corps founded
1934
Federal Radio Commission becomes Federal Communications Commission
Securities and Exchange Commission established
Federal Savings and Loan Insurance Corporation established
Sen. Huey Long and Dr. Francis E. Townsend each propose radical income redistribution plans
Harry S. Truman elected U.S. senator from Missouri

President Franklin D. Roosevelt's October 31, 1936, campaign address at Madison Square Garden, New York City continued a New York Democratic Party tradition of holding a rally the Saturday night before elections. With President Roosevelt on the podium are New York Senator Robert F. Wagner and Governor Herbert H. Lehman.

1935
Social Security Act enacted
Italy invades Ethiopia
Nuremberg laws strip German Jews of their citizenship
Anti-Catholic riots in Northern Ireland
Works Progress Administration created
Rural Electrification Administration established to provide power to U.S. rural areas
Eisenhower appointed to Douglas MacArthur's staff in the Philippines
First U.S. public housing project opens in New York

1936
Spanish Civil War begins with military insurgency
Italy annexes Ethiopia
Great Purge begins in the Soviet Union
African-American track star Jesse Owens wins four gold medals at the Olympic Games in Berlin, outraging Hitler

1937
Japan invades China in force, having begun occupation in 1931
Moscow show trials of dissidents begin
German dirigible *Hindenberg* explodes over Lakehurst, New Jersey
U.S. pioneer aviator Amelia Earhart disappears
Nylon patented

1938
Hitler annexes Austria and takes the Sudetenland in Czechoslovakia
Jewish property and lives are destroyed in German *Kristallnacht* riots
U.S. Food, Drug, and Cosmetic Act passed

1939
Germany invades Poland; World War II begins
Spanish Civil War ends with fall of Madrid
Soviets invade Finland
Turmoil in Palestine causes British to repudiate Balfour Declaration of 1917

1940
Holland, Luxembourg, Denmark, Belgium, and France fall to the Germans
First peacetime draft begins in U.S.
1941
Lend-Lease Act provides aid to Allied effort
Germany invades Russia
U.S. enters war after Japan bombs Pearl Harbor
John F. Kennedy joins U.S. Navy
1942
Doolittle raid on Tokyo
Rommel offensive in North Africa
Battle of Stalingrad begins
MacArthur placed in command in Southwest Pacific; Chester Nimitz in remainder of Pacific; Eisenhower in North Africa
Office of Strategic Services created
U.S. rations gas, sugar, coffee
Richard Nixon, Gerald Ford join U.S. Navy
1943
Eisenhower put in command of Allied forces in Europe
Allies invade Italy
Wage and price freezes
Coal industry nationalized
1944
RAF raid on Berlin
Allies take Rome
Eisenhower leads D-Day Normandy invasion
Charles de Gaulle enters Paris
Guam captured
Battle of the Bulge
G.I. Bill provides support for education of veterans and for low-cost home loans

Harry S. Truman, 1945-1953
1945
FDR dies; Vice President Harry S. Truman succeeds
Mussolini executed
Hitler commits suicide
Germany surrenders
Atomic bomb dropped on Hiroshima
V-J Day proclaimed and World War II ends, having taken more than 54 million lives
United Nations established
Penicillin first used commercially
1946
United Nations General Assembly meets
"Iron Curtain" speech by Churchill
Britain establishes National Health Plan
Massive strikes in U.S.; coal industry temporarily taken over by federal government
Richard Nixon elected to Congress
Jimmy Carter graduates from the U.S. Naval Academy
Bill Clinton born

1947
George Marshall appointed Secretary of State.
Truman Doctrine supports fight against communism
Taft-Hartley Act passed
Central Intelligence Agency established
Herbert Hoover coordinates postwar European food relief program
1948
Marshall Plan enacted
U.S.S.R. cuts off traffic to West Berlin; West begins airlift of food and supplies
Jewish state of Israel established and is recognized by President Truman
Apartheid established in South Africa
Gandhi assassinated by Hindu extremists
U.S. railroads taken over by Army to evade strike
Lyndon B. Johnson elected U.S. senator from Texas
1949
Communist People's Republic of China established
North Atlantic Treaty Organization created
Soviets develop atomic bomb
Creation of East and West Germany
Richard Nixon elected to U.S. Senate
Gerald Ford elected to Congress
1950
North Korea invades South Korea; UN forces sent to South Korea
Joseph McCarthy claims U.S. State Department is riddled with Communists, begins a period of Communist "witch hunts"
1951
22nd Amendment: President limited to two terms of office
MacArthur relieved of his duties in Korea
Julius and Ethel Rosenberg found guilty of selling atomic secrets to the Soviet Union
1952
U.S. explodes a hydrogen thermonuclear bomb
Truman seizes steel mills in response to strike
Accused of campaign finance improprieties, vice-presidential candidate Richard Nixon delivers a convincing denial on television, the "Checkers speech"
John F. Kennedy elected to U.S. Senate from Massachusetts

Dwight D. Eisenhower, 1953-1961
1953
U.S.S.R. explodes hydrogen bomb
Julius and Ethel Rosenberg executed
Korean War ends
Charlie Chaplin denied entrance into U.S. because of his leftist politics
Lyndon B. Johnson becomes Democratic leader in Senate
1954
Brown vs. Board of Education decision by the Supreme Court overturns "separate but equal" doctrine, leading toward desegregation
France asks for aid from U.S. in its fight against communists in Vietnam and is denied
Bikini tests of hydrogen bomb
1955
AFL-CIO merge (American Federation of Labor and Congress of Industrial Organizations)
Civil war in South Vietnam

1956
Egypt seizes Suez canal; UN intervenes
Hungarian uprising against Soviets quelled by U.S.S.R. troops
Interstate Highway System given massive support by federal government
1957
Eisenhower sends federal paratroopers to Little Rock, Arkansas, to enforce integration of Central High School
U.S.S.R. launches Sputnik I & II, the first man-made satellites
1958
Fidel Castro battles dictator Fulgencio Batista in Cuba
U.S. launches Explorer I satellite
1959
Castro becomes Premier of Cuba after Batista flees
Vice President Nixon and Soviet Premier Nikita Khrushchev "debate" in a model-kitchen exhibition in Moscow
Alaska becomes the 49th state, Hawaii the 50th
1960
Francis Gary Powers' U-2 spy plane shot down over U.S.S.R.
Birth control pill approved by the FDA

John F. Kennedy, 1961-63
1961
23rd Amendment: District of Columbia residents given right to vote in presidential elections
U.S. relations severed with Cuba; U.S.'s Bay of Pigs invasion fails
Berlin Wall built
U.S.S.R. cosmonaut orbits earth; U.S. sends first astronaut into space
Civil rights Freedom Riders arrested and beaten
Function and structure of DNA revealed by James Dewey Watson and Francis Crick
1962
Cuban missile crisis
U.S. sends astronauts into orbit
Silent Spring by Rachel Carson published; exposes dangers of DDT pesticide
African-American James Meredith enters the University of Mississippi under federal protection
1963
Civil rights march on Washington is highlighted by Rev. Martin Luther King Jr.'s "I have a dream" speech

Lyndon B. Johnson, 1963-1969
1964
24th Amendment: Poll tax outlawed in federal elections
Gulf of Tonkin resolution begins escalation of U.S. involvement in Vietnam
Major civil rights legislation passed
U.S. Surgeon General report reaffirms link between cigarette smoking and lung cancer
1965
Vietnam war escalation
Selma to Montgomery, Alabama, civil rights march
Black Muslim leader Malcolm X assassinated
Medicare enacted
Riots in Watts, Los Angeles
COMSAT launches "Early Bird" communications satellite
National Endowment for the Arts and National Endowment for the Humanities created

1966
Cultural Revolution in China
U.S. bombing of North Vietnam
Medicare program goes into effect
Miranda Supreme Court decision
Ronald Reagan elected governor of California
1967
25th Amendment: Presidential succession rules changed
Arab-Israeli Six-Day war
China explodes hydrogen bomb
First heart transplant operation
Race riots in many U.S. cities
Thurgood Marshall named to Supreme Court: First African-American on court
1968
Rev. Martin Luther King Jr. assassinated
Robert F. Kennedy assassinated
Soviets invade Czechoslovakia
Rioting at Democratic National Convention
Campus protests of Vietnam War

Richard M. Nixon, 1969-1974
1969
Mass demonstrations against Vietnam War
Apollo 11 lands two Americans on the moon
1970
U.S. bombs Vietcong supply routes in Cambodia; fighting spreads to Laos and Cambodia
National Guard troops kill four students demonstrating at Kent State University against
    U.S. involvement in Vietnam
University of Wisconsin protesters blow up a university laboratory, killing a graduate student
First "Earth Day"
Environmental Protection Agency created by Congress
Jimmy Carter elected governor of Georgia

Not all the silent majority was silent. One Nixon fan actually wanted to be a drug agent.

1971
26th Amendment: Federal and state election voting age lowered to 18
U.S. Supreme Court upholds busing of schoolchildren to desegregate schools
Riots at Attica Correctional Facility, New York
1972
President Nixon visits China
Democratic National Headquarters at Washington Watergate complex burglarized
1973
Cover-up of Watergate-related activities forces several White House aides to resign
Vice President Spiro T. Agnew resigns
Arab-Israeli Yom Kippur War
OPEC oil embargo spurs energy crisis
Supreme Court's Roe v. Wade ruling legalizes abortion
U.S. involvement in Vietnam ends
1974
Inflation and recession
White House staff members convicted
President's tape recordings released
President Nixon resigns; Vice President Gerald Ford becomes President

Gerald Ford, 1974-1977
1974
Ford pardons Nixon
1975
Saigon seized by communists
1976
Washington and Moscow sign treaty limiting underground nuclear testing
U.S. celebrates Bicentennial

President Jimmy Carter, July 15, 1979.

Jimmy Carter, 1977-1981

1977
Treaty relinquishing U.S. ownership of Panama Canal negotiated

1978
California voters approve Proposition 13 resulting in 57% property tax cut
U.S. Senate ratifies new Panama Canal treaties
Menachem Begin and Anwar Sadat meet to begin work on an Israeli-Egyptian peace treaty

1979
Ayatollah Khomeini leads fundamentalist government in Iran; U.S. Embassy staff and Marines taken hostage
SALT II arms limitation treaty signed by U.S. and U.S.S.R.
Three Mile Island nuclear power plant accident
Soviets invade Afghanistan

1980
Carter boycotts 1980 Olympics and imposes a grain embargo
Rise of Solidarity movement in Poland
Iran-Iraq war

Ronald Reagan, 1981-1989

1981
Assassination attempt on President Reagan
Fifty-two hostages released in Iran
AIDS identified
IBM PC introduced

1982
Sinai returned to Egypt by Israel
First heart transplant

1983
President Reagan proposes the Strategic Defense Initiative ("Star Wars") defense system
U.S. invades Grenada to reverse leftist military coup

1984
U.S. launches space shuttle *Discovery*

1985
U.S. imposes limited sanctions against South Africa to protest Apartheid
Gorbachev becomes premier of U.S.S.R.

1986
U.S. admits to secret arms deal with Iran
Challenger space shuttle explodes after take-off
Glasnost and perestroika movements restore social freedoms in U.S.S.R.

1987
First trillion-dollar U.S. budget
U.S. signs INF missile treaty with Soviet Union
Dow Jones average falls 23% on "Black Monday"

1988
U.S. and Canada sign Free Trade Agreement

George Bush, 1989-1993

1989
Chinese military massacres pro-democracy demonstrators in Tiananmen Square
U.S. invades Panama, installs new government
Reunification of East and West Germany

1990
Iraq invades Kuwait
Solidarity leaders, Lech Walesa elected President of Poland
1991
U.S. and allies drive Iraq from Kuwait
Dow Jones average climbs above 3000
U.S. Senate, after acrimonious hearings regarding charges of sexual harassment, approves the nomination of Clarence Thomas to the U.S. Supreme Court
Failure of Soviet coup brings an end to the Soviet Union; Boris Yeltsin becomes the president of Russian federation
1992
Riots in Los Angeles following acquittal of police officers accused of beating Rodney King
U.S. troops sent to Somalia

Bill Clinton, 1993-
1993
North American Free Trade Agreement ratified
1994
Major earthquake in Los Angeles
U.S. troops land in Haiti
Nelson Mandela sworn in as South Africa's first black president
Self-rule established in Israeli occupied territories
Unsuccessful effort by Clinton to establish health care reform
Fighting breaks out in Rwanda
Republican majority elected to U.S. Senate and House of Representatives
1995
Republican *Contract with America* guides legislative agenda in Congress
Trial of O.J. Simpson

Other Rhino titles you may enjoy:

Great Speeches Of The 20th Century, Vol. 1: Presidential Addresses (#71812)
Great Speeches Of The 20th Century, Vol. 2: The New Frontier (#71813)
Great Speeches Of The 20th Century, Vol. 3: Dreams And Realities (#71814)
Great Speeches Of The 20th Century [Expanded 4 Vol. Box Set] (#70567)

GET ON THE RHINO MAILING LIST Receive our special MAIL ORDER catalog featuring over a thousand critically acclaimed Rhino compact discs and cassettes. Send one dollar (check or money order, payable to Rhino Records Inc.) along with your name and address to: Rhino Catalog, 10635 Santa Monica Blvd., Los Angeles, CA 90025-4900.

What your mama didn't tell you, and what we want you to know is, you could be *Shopping For A Better World*.

Every time we step up to a cash register, we vote. If you want your purchases to reflect your principles, you should know about *Shopping For A Better World*. This publication of the Council on Economic Priorities rates 186 companies that make 2,400 brand name products on 10 social issues. You can use it to help you select products made by companies whose policies and practices you support.

So the next time you're checking out a product for quality and price, why not also check out the social performance of the company behind the product? Turn your shopping cart into a vehicle for social change.

For more information on how you can join nearly 1,000,000 people who are shopping for a better world, please write or call:

COUNCIL ON ECONOMIC PRIORITIES
30 Irving Place
New York, NY 10003
(800) 729-4237